I0886530

Lectionary Mosaics

Lectionary Mosaics

Three Readings Juxtaposed for Reflection and Proclamation

Gordon W. Lathrop

AUGSBURG FORTRESS
MINNEAPOLIS

LECTIONARY MOSAICS
Three Readings Juxtaposed for Reflection and Proclamation

Cover design: Josh Eller
Cover image: Mausoleum of Galla Placidia, Ravenna, Italy.
Photo copyright © Borisb17/Getty Images Plus via Getty Images.
Interior design and typesetting: Josh Eller
Editor: Jennifer Baker-Trinity
Manufactured in the U.S.A.

pISBN 978-1-5064-8601-7
eISBN 978-1-5064-9518-7

30 29 28 27 26 25 24 23 1 2 3 4 5 6 7 8 9 10

Contents

	Introduction	1
1.	Readings for Festivals with Only One Set: Christmas to Epiphany	9
2.	Readings for Festivals with Only One Set: Ash Wednesday, the Three Days, and Ascension	13
3.	Readings for Year A	19
4.	Readings for Year B	55
5.	Readings for Year C	95
6.	Readings for Lesser Festivals When Observed on Sunday	135

Introduction

The three-year ecumenical lectionary presents Christians with a treasure that can deepen preaching in their assemblies, present those assemblies with a rich and diverse banquet of scripture, and enliven biblical reflection when people are alone or at home with others. The paragraphs written here about each set of lectionary readings are intended to help with all those projects: reading at home, preparing for worship, and specifically preparing to preach.

This collection of such paragraphs is based upon the Revised Common Lectionary (RCL), the most widely used lectionary in the ecumenical world today. Still, this book and its reflections can also be helpful more widely—among Christians whose churches have adopted but slightly revised the RCL, and also among Roman Catholic Christians whose three-year lectionary formed the original basis for the RCL, though the RCL has sometimes diverged from that source, especially in regard to the length of the readings.

The deep conviction alive in this book is that the RCL, its denominational variants, and the Roman Lectionary all share the same goal: that the scriptures be read in the assembly on Sunday to proclaim the crucified and risen Jesus Christ and to enable the encounter in him with the very presence of the grace of the triune God for the life of the world. These lectionary texts are intended to be read at eucharist and to be read in remembrance of baptism. The same Spirit that enlivens the bath and the meal gives us life in these words. The same Jesus Christ into whose death we have been baptized, who gives his own body and blood in the bread and cup, also gives himself away in the readings.

The same Father of Jesus to whom we give thanks at the font and the table speaks here in these expressions of the word of God. The texts of the lectionary enable us to know who it is in whom we die and rise in baptism, who it is whom we encounter and receive in the holy communion. Preachers do well to use the readings to make this triune God known and to invite people to eat and drink the gospel they have heard, the same gospel that was washed over them in baptism.

This ecumenical three-year lectionary has sometimes been compared to a banquet: the churches in using it have determined to set out richer fare, more diverse material from the Bible, a several-course feast, the various readings being seen as those courses. Just as Ezekiel and John the elder both were given a scroll to eat and then were sent to speak (Ezek. 2:8—3:3; Rev. 10:8-10), so we too—and especially our preacher—may "eat" God's word, finding there both the "lamentation and mourning and woe" of our needy world and the sweetness of the life-giving gospel. Our assemblies are to live from this feast.

This lectionary might also be compared to a mosaic. Diversely colored and jewel-like bits of glass or stone (*tesserae*) are put together. Juxtaposed to each other, they can make one image. With the *tesserae* used carefully, the image will show us the presence here of the triune God centered in the presence of Jesus Christ. Our assemblies are to find their purpose in that presence. The cover of this book includes one such image: a mosaic from the mausoleum of Galla Placidia in Ravenna, Italy. The monogram at the top center represents the Greek letters for *Chr*, thus for Christ. The Alpha and Omega can represent that the risen Christ is the beginning and the end of all things, or they can represent God who was the beginning of all things and the Spirit of God coming to us now from the end. Amid the swirling vines around and below that monogram and beneath the thin stone window letting in the light, two deer drink from a fountain. The mosaic, like the paragraphs in this book, stands for the presence of the living and life-giving God from whose word we drink: "As the deer longs for the water-brooks, so longs my soul for you, O God" (Ps. 42:1).

Both images, banquet and mosaic, urge us to pay attention to all three readings. We ought not omit the gift of one of the courses of the feast, or we may go hungry. We cannot leave out some of the bits of glass or stone, or the image will be unclear or even absent. In a faithful liturgy, all three readings will have been proclaimed in our hearing. We do well to think about all three together. Our preacher will do well to preach amid the echoes in the room from all three.

Nonetheless, we cannot always meet in assembly or gather around the eucharist. Most of the lectionary paragraphs collected in this present book were originally written during the great coronavirus pandemic, when care about our neighbors, especially about the spread of disease to the most vulnerable among us, required that we not meet together in person at all. The scriptures were still available to us, however, and many Christians read the Sunday lectionary at home. The sentences written here were originally intended to help people at home encounter the risen Christ in the readings in a time when the full assembly was impossible. Such a time may return. Even more, there will always be personal times when sickness or distance or imprisonment keeps us from the assembly. The lectionary can still be there for us, speaking grace into our lives. "We eat the flesh and drink the blood of the divine Savior in the holy eucharist," said the fourth-century biblical scholar Jerome, "but so do we in the reading of the scriptures."

Each of these paragraphs, then, is intended for any preacher preparing to preach in the assembly, as a few beginning ideas for that preparation. The paragraphs are not themselves sermons; they are meant to be little mosaics showing one way that the stones of the readings might be patterned together to image the presence of Jesus Christ in the assembly. Each of these paragraphs is also intended for the lector preparing to read, for the assisting minister or deacon preparing the intercessions, and for all of us, simply preparing to go to church. Reading the readings ahead of time and reflecting on how they work together can be a splendid preparation for worship participation, a grounding preparation for interceding for the world, and a focusing preparation for the ministry of public reading. The paragraphs are also, at the same time, intended for the isolated Christian or group of Christians enacting a memory of assembly, reading the lectionary in a sort of domestic church, when they cannot join the assembly itself.

With such purposes in mind, you will find several characteristics of the lectionary accentuated in these paragraphs. For one thing, there are three readings in every lectionary set except the set for the great Vigil of Easter, and there one hears between six and fourteen readings, depending on local choice. How the readings are juxtaposed to each other—the diverse ways their multiple voices speak together—these are among the most important and joyful discoveries of lectionary study. The major concern of the paragraphs here is that juxtaposition of the three texts. So, again, I have aimed for each paragraph to be a small mosaic.

I am quite aware that such an approach may be seen as new—even contrary to what some pastors have been taught about preaching as attending to the unique circumstances of any one text, apart from the others. I simply ask you to consider what is here outlined as an alternate way. The assembly is not a Bible study. It is a gathering in the presence of Jesus Christ, drawing us into the life of the triune God and turning us toward the needs of the world. I think the lectionary can best be seen as serving that purpose when the three readings are viewed together.

Here are two biblical images for what is proposed: It is as if the readings were all working together—like the living creatures of Revelation 4 and 5, the quite diverse living creatures, surrounding the throne of God and of the Lamb and calling out their praise. Or it is as if the readings were like the two golden cherubim on the lid of the ark in Exodus 25, between which the living God encountered Israel from what was called "the mercy seat." In, among, and between the readings—at every Sunday and festival—we meet the living God, we find the mercy seat, we encounter the Lamb who was slain, now standing and alive.

"The Lamb who was slain": the lectionary is always about the crucified and risen Christ. For us, the Crucified and Risen One is where we find the mercy seat of God. Just as Paul, the source of the great majority of the second readings in the RCL, determined "to know nothing" among the churches "except Jesus Christ, and him crucified" (1 Cor. 2:2), so the lectionary has determined. Just as the gospels find that every story of Jesus has lines that run on to the end of the book, to the passion and resurrection narrative of that gospel book, so the lectionary uses the gospel reading. Every gospel reading becomes a resurrection appearance now, with Christ showing us his wounds. Indeed, stories of the life and ministry of Jesus are read to us as images of what Jesus Christ in the power of the Spirit is doing among us now: healing, forgiving, teaching, welcoming, raising the dead. And taught by the way the New Testament is so strongly built out of imagery from the Old Testament, the lectionary borrows that imagery repeatedly, using the first reading to show us the meaning of the gospel of God amid our failure and hope.

More: with Isaiah, when we encounter the living God, as we do in reading the scriptures, we may say, "Woe is me! I am lost" (Isa. 6:5). The scriptures not infrequently accuse us. And they always give us images for our utter need and the need of the whole world: "lamentation and mourning and woe" (Ezek. 2:10). But much more than that accusation and that accurate description of need, they pour out the restoring and life-giving mercy of God. The three-year lectionary gives us, Sunday after Sunday, sometimes more in one reading than another, but always all together, words of law and words of gospel: descriptions of our failure, sin, and need, and the very gift of God's mercy.

And to trust in that mercy, to let our faith in God be awakened again, to thus be united with the risen Christ, inevitably means to turn to our neighbor in loving service. The lectionary encourages us, as Paul says, toward "faith working through love" (Gal. 5:6). And awakening us to faith again, to trust in God, is another way to speak of the core purpose of reading the lectionary in assembly.

In each mosaic paragraph that follows here you will find then, briefly set out,

- ideas about how all three readings can be made to speak together, both in tension and in concert;
- seriousness about the critical reading of the scriptures, including the awareness that there are four gospels, each with a different voice;
- the texts of the lectionary always seen as proclaiming the ministry, the cross, the resurrection, and the assembly presence of Jesus Christ;
- the texts as a doorway into the life of the holy Trinity—that is, into the life of God as known in Christ;
- the texts as materials the Holy Spirit may use to call us again to faith, to enable us to trust God;
- the texts seen as both law and gospel, both judgment and hope;
- the texts as celebrating the meaning of Sunday—the resurrection of Christ and the assembly gathered around the Risen One—and the meaning of the great seasons: human longing for God in Advent, the incarnation in Christmas and Epiphany, baptism in Lent, and yet again the resurrection in the fifty days of Easter;
- ways in which the readings can be seen as illumining at least one of the sacraments: baptism—along with absolution, the return to baptism—and eucharist; and
- the call to turn with Christ in love toward the needs of those around us.

Each paragraph is prefaced by the name of the Sunday or festival or, in the case of the standard Sundays—the Sundays between Baptism of Our Lord and Transfiguration, and the Sundays between Holy Trinity and Christ the King—the lectionary or proper number, two different ways the lectionary sets are designated in the diverse churches. Then the readings are listed, beginning with the gospel for the day. That order does not represent the order of reading in the liturgy but the symbolic priority of the text that most especially stands for Jesus Christ risen. The psalm is included, along with the antiphon proposed for that psalm in *Evangelical Lutheran Worship*. The psalm is not a reading but a communal sung response to the first reading, though its antiphon frequently provides both a key to that psalm and a way to reflect deeply on all the readings together. In this book, the first reading is always drawn from the "complementary series" on the standard Sundays. The semicontinuous option makes the construction of an assembly-purposed mosaic much more difficult. Sometimes the RCL, on various Sundays and festivals, has yet other options for one or the other of the readings. This book has made a choice, hoping the sentences will still be useful to you even if that particular reading is not your assembly's choice.

The book is primarily organized around the three years. However, some major festivals have the same readings in all three years. Rather than print the paragraphs for those festivals three times, they were gathered together in the two chapters at the beginning of the book, one for the Christmas cycle and one for the Lent and Easter cycle. Furthermore, in the use of *Evangelical Lutheran Worship*, there are some lesser festivals that, if they occur on Sunday, can bring their own readings to replace the given readings for the Sunday. The lesser festivals that often (though not necessarily) replace the Sunday readings are Name of Jesus; Presentation of Our Lord; Reformation Day; and All Saints Day. The lesser festivals which may, by local choice, replace the standard Sunday readings are John the Baptist; Peter and Paul, Apostles; Mary, Mother of Our Lord; Holy Cross Day; and Michael and All Angels. All of these lectionary sets, except for All Saints Day, are considered together in the final chapter. All Saints Day has three sets of readings, one in each of the three years. These readings are then considered in their place in years A, B, and C.

Of course, much more could be—and has been—written about these texts. Three readings together leave a lot of room for interpretation. These mosaics simply present one way to see them meaningfully juxtaposed. People who read the texts when alone, or preachers and readers who are preparing to read or preach in the assembly, are urged to do much wider reading: biblical exegesis, denominational and ecumenical resources about the lectionary, books about liturgical meaning, books about preaching. Those living with these texts are also urged to read regular sources of the news, so to juxtapose the texts to events in our time. They are also urged to read the natural world around us and to see how the earth-loving character of the scriptures invites us to care about that earth.

Still, the special concern here has been to briefly indicate the importance of more than one text, the ways that a juxtaposition of readings enriches us, and the essential assembly purpose of the three-year lectionaries. A further rationale for what is included in these paragraphs can be found especially in my *Proclaiming the Living Word: A Handbook for Preachers* (Minneapolis: Augsburg Fortress, 2018).

May these little word-mosaics be helpful to you.

Gordon W. Lathrop

A NOTE ON THE CALENDAR

To make use of this book it will be helpful to have access to a church calendar. But with a few pointers, it would be possible for you to construct such a calendar yourself. The Easter cycle stretches from Ash Wednesday to Pentecost and is determined by the date of Easter. The Christmas cycle stretches from the first Sunday of Advent to Epiphany and is determined by the date of Christmas. The date of Easter in the Western churches is the first Sunday after the first full moon after the vernal equinox. Six Sundays in Lent precede Easter. Ash Wednesday, the beginning of Lent, is the Wednesday before the first Sunday in Lent. Easter is fifty days long and includes eight Sundays, the first being Easter Day itself, the eighth being Pentecost. Christmas, celebrated on December 25, is preceded by four Sundays of Advent and followed by Epiphany on January 6 as well as the one or two Sundays that occur between Christmas and Epiphany.

The lectionary, then is organized in three years:

- Year A begins on the First Sunday of Advent in 2022, 2025, 2028, 2031, and every three years after that.
- Year B begins on the First Sunday of Advent in 2023, 2026, 2029, 2032, and every three years after that.
- Year C begins on the First Sunday of Advent in 2024, 2027, 2030, 2033, and every three years after that.

The first Sunday after Epiphany is celebrated as Baptism of Our Lord, and the lectionary numbering begins on that day with Lectionary 1. The standard Sundays using these numbered lectionary sets, both after Epiphany and after Pentecost, are also dated within a range of dates so that they can be easily found. The last Sunday after Epiphany, the Sunday just before Ash Wednesday, is celebrated as Transfiguration of Our Lord. The Sunday after Pentecost is celebrated as the festival of the Holy Trinity. The numbered lectionary sets and the dated standard Sundays then begin again after Holy Trinity and continue to the end of the year, the Sunday before Advent begins. That Sunday is kept as the festival Christ the King.

CHAPTER 1

Readings for Festivals with Only One Set

Christmas to Epiphany

NATIVITY OF OUR LORD I, CHRISTMAS EVE

Luke 2:1-14
Isaiah 9:2-7
Psalm 96 Let the heavens rejoice and the earth be glad. (Ps. 96:11)
Titus 2:11-14

Having read these readings, consider this:

Jesus Christ is the light that shines in the darkness, the grace of God that has appeared among us, the Prince of peace in a warring world. This night we celebrate all these things, knowing our own need for them. Our liturgy uses an old Israelite text from Isaiah, probably originally spoken at the enthronement of a local king. But no king ever fulfilled what was spoken in that text. Rather, it is in Jesus Christ that there is a promise of the end of burdens placed on oppressed people and the end of garments rolled in blood. The gospel tells of the reign of the Roman emperor, evidencing how he violently pushed people around. But the child whose birth is told in this story has his bed among the poor in their need, sharing their weakness. In contrast with Augustus, a far more profound authority for "all the world" belongs to him. In the end, this Jesus Christ reigns from the cross and brings peace in his resurrection. The story says there was no room for him in the place for guests and travelers. By the power of the Spirit and with Mary, we rightly welcome him, this story, and his meal-gift into our hearts. We rightly labor for justice for the poor, whose life he shared.

NATIVITY OF OUR LORD III, CHRISTMAS DAY

John 1:1-14
Isaiah 52:7-10
Psalm 98 All the ends of the earth have seen the victory of our God. (Ps. 98:3)
Hebrews 1:1-4

Having read these readings, consider this:

"All the ends of the earth shall see the salvation of our God." Today, on a brief, bright winter day, on a quiet festive day, we enter into that seeing. That victory and salvation come here, to this end of the earth, for us to behold with our eyes. Jesus Christ "is the reflection of God's glory and the exact imprint of God's very being." Word of God become flesh, living among us, "we have seen his glory, . . . full of grace and truth." On this Christmas Day we see him and his salvation: in the word we read; in the assembly around this word and in the bread and cup where he gives himself away, or in the treasured memory of that assembly and that meal; in the faces of people who belong to him and are near to us; in our neighbors; in the very earth that came into being through him and holds together in him. Look at the Word become flesh and rejoice, receiving that fullness of grace and truth. Resolve to care for that earth.

FIRST SUNDAY OF CHRISTMAS

See below, in year A, B, or C, as appropriate.

SECOND SUNDAY OF CHRISTMAS

John 1:10-18
Jeremiah 31:7-14
Psalm 147:12-20 Worship the Lord, O Jerusalem; praise your God, O Zion. (Ps. 147:12)
Ephesians 1:3-14

Having read these readings, consider this:

In some years we keep Sunday a second time in the days of Christmas, and the whole mystery of the incarnation of God in Christ washes over us again. Of course, we are often part of that world that does not know him, his own people who do not accept him. But the Word is given to us in these readings. As we receive it, the Spirit of God comes to us, and we are brought to faith again. We welcome into our hearts and lives Jesus Christ, incarnate, crucified, and risen; the very one who has shared our nature and our lot; the very light that illumines all things. Then, as we rightly weep about the needs of ourselves and others, God meets us with consolations. Hearing the word together with all the church, we are made a watered garden; a place of grain, wine, and oil in the sacraments; a rescued city; a people of the light. In the Word, which is the very presence of Christ, we receive grace upon grace. We are renewed to turn with this same news to our neighbors and to all the suffering earth.

EPIPHANY OF OUR LORD, JANUARY 6

Matthew 2:1-12
Isaiah 60:1-6
Psalm 72:1-7, 10-14 All kings shall bow down before him. (Ps. 72:11)
Ephesians 3:1-12

Having read these readings, consider this:

Herod has a way to see the world: it is centered on himself, his power, his privileges, his city. He is willing to lie and kill to keep the world that way. And he consults religious authorities to try to augment this view; after all, he thinks religion has promised that Jerusalem will be the center to which all the nations shall come. We may often be like Herod, centered on ourselves, using religion only for our own purposes. But if we will listen, this story reconstructs our world. The magi, representing those many nations, do come. But the light they see leads them finally not to the city but to a village, not to a palace but to a house, not to a king but to a child, and their gifts foretell this child's death. The child, grown to be our crucified and risen Lord Jesus, the very mystery of God revealed, draws us and all things into God. There is the center: Jesus Christ, the presence and glory of God. That center is present wherever this word is heard: every house of the church in all the world, when we can gather; our very own homes, when the scripture is read and we pray for all the nations; the places of our needy neighbors, with whom Christ identifies. Let the star of these texts lead you. They will show you a whole new way to see the world, one centered on God, not on us. "Arise, shine; for your light has come."

CHAPTER 2

Readings for Festivals with Only One Set

Ash Wednesday, the Three Days, and Ascension

ASH WEDNESDAY

Matthew 6:1-6, 16-21
Joel 2:1-2, 12-17
Psalm 51:1-17 Have mercy on me, O God, according to your steadfast love. (Ps. 51:1)
2 Corinthians 5:20b—6:10

Having read these readings, consider this:

On Ash Wednesday, with a day of fasting and repentance, we begin our forty-day journey toward Easter. Letting our foreheads be marked with dust or ashes, we acknowledge that we die and return to the earth. At the same time, the mark traces the life-giving cross that was indelibly placed on our foreheads at baptism. While we journey through Lent to return to God, we have already been reconciled to God through Christ. We humbly pray for God to make our hearts clean while we rejoice that "now is the day of salvation." Returning to our baptismal call, we more intentionally bear the fruits of mercy and justice in the world.

SUNDAY OF THE PASSION, PALM SUNDAY

(A) Matthew 21:1-11 and Matthew 26:14—27:66
(B) Mark 11:1-11 and Mark 14:1—15:47
(C) Luke 19:28-40 and Luke 22:14—23:56
Isaiah 50:4-9a
Psalm 31:9-16 Into your hands, O LORD, I commend my spirit. (Ps. 31:5)
Philippians 2:5-11

When you have read the palm procession gospel, consider this:

When in the past we have read this text in church and carried the palm branches, we were celebrating the presence of Jesus Christ coming among us as we began all the services of this Holy Week. If you are not able to join the gathering, you may trust that Christ comes also now to your home, to be with you in the word as you begin this week of prayer, apart but together with the whole church. If you are able to be part of the assembly, remember the times when you could not, and rejoice, praying also for those who are absent. Blessed indeed is the One who comes!

When you have read the other Passion Sunday texts consider this:

As the psalm today says, fear is certainly all around. This story of the suffering of Christ powerfully fits our time, and we can recognize ourselves in the fearful crowd, if not also in the betrayers and killers. But why does God in Christ enter into such agonies? To plant hope and life and God's very self deep in all human suffering, so that from now on there is no place of hurt and sorrow where Jesus Christ is not there first. To defeat all dread and death, so that we might no longer live in fear. By the work of the Spirit, to plant the mind of Christ in us, so that we might turn to our neighbor in love.

Then note: In Mark, Jesus suffers and dies, yet in his suffering, paradoxically he drinks the cup of the reign of God arriving, and in his death the temple curtain is torn open. In Matthew, the Markan account of Christ's suffering is repeated and intensified, with the suicide of Judas and the guard at the tomb, yet this Suffering One could call on twelve legions of angels, and his death gives life to those in the tombs. And in Luke, Jesus is mocked also by Herod, but his death is the source of forgiveness and the welcome to the thief. All of these paradoxical gifts of the cross are present for us in the word and in the Sunday assembly: the reign of God now; access to the holy; life out of death; welcome to the sinner; and forgiveness.

MAUNDY THURSDAY

John 13:1-17, 31b-35
Exodus 12:1-14
Psalm 116:1-2, 12-19 I will lift the cup of salvation and call on the name of the Lord. (Ps. 116:13)
1 Corinthians 11:23-26

Having read these readings, consider this:

This word about the love of Jesus is always the beginning of any time. By remembering the Passover and the last supper and the footwashing, we are not trying to get back to an old time. In the face of the suffering and death with which the world is filled, our trying would not come to much. But God's word comes to us now. To our time. Even were we not able to meet for the holy supper together, this word—which takes these three nights to say—comes to us. When we are able to meet, this word comes to us in at least three ways. Jesus Christ is our *forgiveness*: he is the Lamb whose blood marks the doors of our houses and bodies. In the power of the Spirit, he has *washed our feet* and our lives, causing us to wash each other. And he does give us himself—his encounterable body, his life-giving blood—in the *supper*. Then he turns us toward our neighbors. In this word—and in the cross proclaimed tomorrow and the resurrection proclaimed on Saturday night—Easter comes out to hold us already.

GOOD FRIDAY

John 18:1—19:42
Isaiah 52:13—53:12
Psalm 22 My God, my God, why have you forsaken me? (Ps. 22:1)
Hebrews 4:14-16; 5:7-9

Having read these readings, consider this:

Jesus Christ is a root out of dry ground. By his wounds we are healed. These paradoxes of Isaiah are echoed in the account in John about his death: he is arrested, yet when he speaks, the soldiers fall down; he is tried, yet he is King, Son of God, and the Man; he is thirsty and dying, yet he is the source of the Spirit and of water and blood to heal us; finally, he is buried, but it is in a garden. All of this means to tell us that God shares our sorrow and need and death, and yet transforms it all to life and salvation and hope. More than just a root out of dry ground, his cross is the great tree of life in which we all may shelter. You may shelter there today. And all those things in all the world that we pray for today, God holds together in Christ.

RESURRECTION OF OUR LORD, VIGIL OF EASTER

The lectionary for the Vigil of Easter calls for four to twelve Old Testament readings, a New Testament reading, and a gospel. An asterisk (*) indicates the scriptures always read. Reflections on each of the readings follow.

*1. Genesis 1:1—2:4a *Creation*
We long for an ordered world. In spite of death and sorrow, the resurrection of Jesus Christ contains the promise of a new creation. Baptized into his death and resurrection, we are made witnesses to God's new order, and it is very good.

2. Genesis 7:1-5, 11-18; 8:6-18; 9:8-13 *Flood*
Our world, many of our leaders, and we ourselves may well deserve the flood from God. But the risen Christ is our ark. The Holy Spirit, the dove that comes to us in our baptism, leads us into a continually renewed life on the earth. Then we may learn to care anew for our neighbors.

3. Genesis 22:1-18 *Testing of Abraham*
Our world still has people who are bound and killed for the sake of religion. But God has indeed provided the lamb: Jesus Christ. In baptism the living God frees us from such religion.

*4. Exodus 14:10-31; 15:20-21 *Deliverance at the Red Sea*
We long for freedom from fear and confusion, sin and death. The resurrection of Christ brings us through the sea to new life, and baptism has enacted that exodus.

*5. Isaiah 55:1-11 *Salvation freely offered to all*
Our very life thirsts—for life, for hope, for God. In the resurrection of Jesus Christ, the water, wine, and milk of God are given away free. And the word in baptism accomplishes God's purpose.

6. Proverbs 8:1-8, 19-21; 9:4b-6 *The wisdom of God*
We are the foolish, in dire need of intelligence, prudence, and understanding. In the resurrection of Jesus Christ, the mercy of God sets out the bread and wine of wisdom. Baptism brings us to that meal tonight and forever.

7. Ezekiel 36:24-28 *A new heart and a new spirit*
   God grant us new and clean hearts! In baptism into the death and resurrection of Christ, the very Spirit of God is poured into us.

8. Ezekiel 37:1-14 *Valley of the dry bones*
   We are the dry bones. The Spirit of God, poured out from Christ's death and resurrection, makes us alive together with him—a whole people standing together in new life, even when we are separated from each other.

9 Zephaniah 3:14-20 *The gathering of God's people*
   Our world is full of disaster and oppression. With the resurrection of Christ, the Lord our God is in our midst. Baptism into him changes shame into praise.

10. Jonah 1:1—2:1 *The deliverance of Jonah*
   We have often run away from our vocation as witnesses to new life, hope, and forgiveness in Christ. His resurrection, like Jonah coming out of the fish after three days—and our baptism into that resurrection, making us like Jonah—restores us to that vocation.

11. Isaiah 61:1-4, 9-11 *Clothed in the garments of salvation*
   Ashes and mourning are often our lot. The Spirit poured out from the death and resurrection of Christ, the Spirit poured into us in baptism, indeed gives a garland and a mantle of praise instead, as if we were clothed for the wedding of God with the earth.

*12. Daniel 3:1-29 *Deliverance from the fiery furnace*
   In our difficult times, we are in the fire. But the crucified and risen Christ is with us in the flames, and we are saved. And Nebuchadnezzar once again does not get it: no one is to be torn limb from limb! God's mercy is for all.

New Testament Reading: Romans 6:3-11
   Having died with Christ in baptism, we will live with him, walking in newness of life, turning in love toward our neighbors.

And after you have read the other readings, read the gospel, and then consider this:

Gospel: John 20:1-18

Mary weeps; so do we. But do not weep—the risen Christ calls each of us by name. And remember the other readings: in him is rescue from the fire, the clothing of salvation, a restored vocation, the end of shame, our dry bones made alive, the source of a new heart, the feast of God's wisdom, the end of thirst, freedom from slavery and fear, the end of bad religion, God's rainbow over the earth, and the very down payment on a new creation. Alleluia! Christ is risen!

RESURRECTION OF OUR LORD, EASTER DAY

See below, in year A, B, or C, as appropriate.

ASCENSION OF OUR LORD, THE FORTIETH DAY OF EASTER

Luke 24:44-53
Acts 1:1-11
Psalm 47 God has gone up with a shout. (Ps. 47:5)
Ephesians 1:15-23

Having read these readings, consider this:

The two men are right. Do not stand looking into the skies as if Jesus has gone away. The Crucified and Risen One has ascended to the throne of God. And where is that? Everywhere, for God's power fills all things. Jesus has ascended into the cosmos. But in a time of sickness and death and loss, that may not be easy to see. Rather, we can see Jesus Christ in the places in which he is there for us: in the scriptures, opening our minds to understand; in the sacraments in the assembly, feeding us; in the Spirit of wisdom, enabling us to hope; and in the love of the community, accompanying us in witness. As Martin Luther has said, Jesus has ascended to be with us and for us. Then we need to be with and for other people, at least in our prayer and support.

DAY OF PENTECOST, THE FIFTIETH DAY OF EASTER

See below, in year A, B, or C, as appropriate.

CHAPTER 3

Readings for Year A

FIRST SUNDAY OF ADVENT

Matthew 24:36-44
Isaiah 2:1-5
Psalm 122 I was glad when they said to me, "Let us go to the house of the LORD." (Ps. 122:1)
Romans 13:11-14

Having read these readings, consider this:

Advent in the northern hemisphere is a time of darkness. Waiting for the light to return becomes for us a metaphor for the widespread human waiting for justice and peace. In Isaiah, God promises to bring all people to the house of the temple to learn the ways of this justice and the paths of this peace, to "walk in the light of the LORD." But we do not know when that promise will be kept. According to Matthew, neither does Jesus. He joins us in waiting, joins us at last from the cross. But by the mercy of God and the gift of the Spirit, the risen Christ is with us now. Our listening to the word of the scriptures and our gathering in the assembly are already the presence of the house of the Lord among us. In baptism and in the holy supper, we put on the Lord Jesus Christ and begin to live again as if it were already full day.

SECOND SUNDAY OF ADVENT

Matthew 3:1-12
Isaiah 11:1-10
Psalm 72:1-7, 18-19 May the righteous flourish; let there be an abundance of peace. (Ps. 72:7)
Romans 15:4-13

Having read these readings, consider this:

John the Baptist each year gives words for our Advent observance, and today in Matthew he speaks law and judgment. We are the trees to be cut down. He also says that the powerful one for whom we wait, the one whom he precedes, will come with fire to clear away the chaff of our unfaithful world. Except, when Jesus does come as that powerful one, it is he who lets himself be cut down with us. Is that the end of hope? On the contrary. Christians believe that the risen Lord Jesus Christ is the root or branch or living tree that grows out of the cut-down stump. The tree of life that we find in him stands as a sign to gather all the peoples of the world. In God's mercy, we ourselves have been welcomed, baptized into his death and life, anointed with the very Holy Spirit that was poured out on him, given the scriptures, and thus brought to hope. Under this tree of life, God continues to prepare the world for which we hope: a world of true justice, profound peace, and widespread knowledge of God. That is our Advent hope. We celebrate it by welcoming others as Christ welcomed us.

THIRD SUNDAY OF ADVENT

Matthew 11:2-11
Isaiah 35:1-10
Psalm 146:5-10 The LORD lifts up those who are bowed down. (Ps. 146:8)
James 5:7-10

Having read these readings, consider this:

In the reading from Matthew this Sunday, John the Baptist, a major biblical voice for us in Advent, is unsure, perhaps even disappointed. He is in prison, about to be killed. How can Jesus be the promised one? This Advent we need to think of all the disappointed ones in the world—the people who wait and wait with no hope: the imprisoned, the war-torn, the chronically ill, the dying.

We may be among them. But Jesus in Matthew answers with scripture, as if his very presence is to be described as Isaiah describes the return from exile: God coming to make a way on which no one will go astray but all the people of deepest need will be saved. This same Jesus is then arrested himself and killed, sharing the lot of John and of all those in deep need. But we must not take offense. Risen and present with the least ones and with us, Jesus Christ again gives us this scripture, like rain on our dry ground. And he gives us himself in the holy meal. By the power of the Spirit, the straight way to life and singing is here, now. The one we meet in word and sacrament is coming still with God's salvation for all. We are called to patience. Let our disappointment be turned to hope and to forbearance with one another.

FOURTH SUNDAY OF ADVENT

Matthew 1:18-25
Isaiah 7:10-16
Psalm 80:1-7, 17-19 Let your face shine upon us, and we shall be saved. (Ps. 80:7)
Romans 1:1-7

Having read these readings, consider this:

On the fourth Sunday of Advent we turn toward Christmas, this year reading the beginning of the story from Matthew. In this version of the announcement of Jesus' birth, quite different from Luke's version, the author of Matthew establishes the theme of the whole gospel book: in Jesus the old oracle spoken by Isaiah to comfort the threatened Ahaz has been fulfilled; in Jesus God is with us. But the birth of Jesus is itself under threat. Mary and her child could have been exposed to shame and even to a cruel death (Deut. 22:20-21). Indeed, in the next story in this gospel, Herod will threaten to kill the child. In Jesus, God is with us amid the sufferings of this world, saving us. We already begin to see the cross. The child grows and, as an adult, is finally killed. But born as son of David, he is declared to be Son of God according to the Holy Spirit by resurrection from the dead. In the power of that Spirit, he is with us still—as Jesus says in the very last words of Matthew: "Remember, I am with you always, to the end of the age" (28:20). In this assembly presence of Jesus, the face of God still shines upon us. Saved, we are called to be saints together, speaking grace and peace for the life of the world.

NATIVITY OF OUR LORD
CHRISTMAS EVE AND CHRISTMAS DAY

See above, in chapter 1.

FIRST SUNDAY OF CHRISTMAS

Matthew 2:13-23
Isaiah 63:7-9
Psalm 148 The splendor of the LORD is over earth and heaven. (Ps. 148:13)
Hebrews 2:10-18

Having read these readings, consider this:

Rachel is still weeping: there are countless places in the world where children and their parents are suffering horribly. The Christmas story makes clear that Jesus Christ has been born amid that sorrow, sharing the suffering of mortal flesh and blood. In contradiction to what has become our holiday excess, we need to note this central theme of the feast, a theme that may help us in openly addressing the hidden sorrow many people feel at Christmas. As Matthew tells the story, Jesus was nearly killed by a fearful tyrant, then was a refugee, and then was finally killed by yet another fearful government. But Christians believe that he has destroyed death and the fear of death by his own death. In him, God's presence is among us and, as the third part of Isaiah says, that presence is saving us and carrying us. By the power of the Spirit in the word of God and in the holy supper, the risen Christ stands in the midst of our assemblies, saying, "Here am I and the children whom God has given me." So held in God's care, we must then turn to do what we can to bear witness to this steadfast love by ourselves holding the weeping ones in our world.

SECOND SUNDAY OF CHRISTMAS

See above, in chapter 1.

EPIPHANY OF OUR LORD

See above, in chapter 1.

BAPTISM OF OUR LORD, FIRST SUNDAY AFTER EPIPHANY
SUNDAY, JANUARY 7–13
LECTIONARY 1

Matthew 3:13-17
Isaiah 42:1-9
Psalm 29 The voice of the LORD is upon the waters. (Ps. 29:3)
Acts 10:34-43

Having read these readings, consider this:

John the Baptist needs to be baptized by Jesus, yet Jesus perseveres in his request. We also need to be baptized by Jesus, while he stands with us in our need. Christians believe that he fulfills the role of the servant spoken of in Second Isaiah, bringing light to the nations and not breaking any of the weak ones of the world. Yet he is himself finally crushed, in spite of the old promise. Still, the Baptized One, the Crucified One, has been raised up. We have now been baptized into him, under the same open heavens, anointed by the same Spirit, called beloved by the same voice of God. The holy Trinity, revealed in the scriptures once again on this day, holds us in mercy and commissions us to join the mission of the Servant. In the assembly, we too eat and drink with the risen Christ. Then we turn to join this same Christ in gently serving—not breaking, not quenching—the needy world.

SECOND SUNDAY AFTER EPIPHANY
SUNDAY, JANUARY 14–20
LECTIONARY 2

John 1:29-42
Isaiah 49:1-7
Psalm 40:1-11 I love to do your will, O my God. (Ps. 40:8)
1 Corinthians 1:1-9

Having read these readings, consider this:

Although John's gospel calls Jesus Christ "the true light, which enlightens everyone" (1:9), in the text for today Jesus is at first hidden. "I myself did not know him," says John the Baptist. Neither did John's disciples. But then, with striking titles, John points him out: Lamb of God; Son of God; the one who baptizes with the Spirit. Jesus tells those disciples to "come and see." They do, and they respond with more titles: Teacher; Messiah. They begin to see who Jesus is. In our time, also, Jesus remains hidden. Many people do not see him. To the world he is dead and gone. And he may be hidden also from us in our lives or our own sorrows. These readings, however, show us that he is hidden like the servant in Isaiah is hidden—in the shadow of God's hand; in God's quiver, ready to be given to all the nations as light. Let us also come and see, for where the risen Christ now stays is with us. We see him as God's Servant in the mutual service of the assembly when we gather. We see him pouring out the Spirit in baptism. We see the Teacher in the scriptures. We see the Lamb of God in the holy supper. And as with Simon, he changes our names and calls us, like the church at Corinth together with all the assemblies in every place, to use our speech and knowledge to bear witness to the mercy of God for every people.

THIRD SUNDAY AFTER EPIPHANY
SUNDAY, JANUARY 21–27
LECTIONARY 3

Matthew 4:12-23
Isaiah 9:1-4
Psalm 27:1, 4-9 The Lord is my light and my salvation. (Ps. 27:1)
1 Corinthians 1:10-18

Having read these readings, consider this:

Every year, in the first Sundays after Epiphany, we hear of Jesus calling the disciples. Last Sunday, with those disciples, we were invited to come and see where Jesus is staying. This Sunday, we hear of fishing for human beings. When we became Christians in baptism, it was as if we were caught in the one great net with all other Christians. We ought not think of ourselves as gathered into separate, fighting factions. Instead, remember this: when fish are caught and pulled into the air, they die. So we were made to die with Christ in baptism. And there is yet more death in the texts today: the part of Galilee where Jesus moves has been a land of great suffering in warfare; John is arrested and will be killed; and beginning to preach, Jesus starts the movement that will lead to his death. Still, Christians believe that the word about his cross is the very power of God. More: Christians believe that the old royal oracle we read from Isaiah is to be understood as speaking of Jesus Christ crucified and risen to be light for every hurt place in the world, that our death with Christ has made us alive together with him, that the Spirit poured out from him is bringing us all to unity, and that we now can assist in taking the yoke and the rod off the necks of our neighbors.

FOURTH SUNDAY AFTER EPIPHANY *(if before Transfiguration)* SUNDAY, JANUARY 28–FEBRUARY 3 LECTIONARY 4

Matthew 5:1-12
Micah 6:1-8
Psalm 15 LORD, who may abide upon your holy hill? (Ps.15:1)
1 Corinthians 1:18-31

Having read these readings, consider this:

On this Sunday we begin to read from the Sermon on the Mount, and the beatitudes stand at the outset of this first of the five discourses in Matthew. As beautiful as these sayings are, they also accuse us. We are often not merciful, pure in heart, or any other of the countercultural characteristics extolled here. The text from Micah also accuses us, as if God has a court case against us. In spite of God's repeated, liberating mercy, we frequently turn away from doing justice and loving kindness. But Paul has words for us that help: Jesus Christ, who went to the cross, shows the paradoxical character of God's wisdom. Against the expectation of the world, Christ crucified is our wisdom and righteousness. Then we see that Christ himself embodies the beatitudes: in his ministry and in his death he was poor with the poor, mourning with the mourning, merciful and peacemaking. In his resurrection he is the presence of all of God's blessedness among us. Now, though we may not be of great status in the world, we are called into life in him, baptized into his cross and resurrection. The Spirit of God, poured out from him, enables us to turn to our neighbors with justice and mercy. God does not need our sacrifices. But in the assembly God gives us mercy, that we might show mercy.

FIFTH SUNDAY AFTER EPIPHANY *(if before Transfiguration)* SUNDAY, FEBRUARY 4–10 LECTIONARY 5

Matthew 5:13-20
Isaiah 58:1-12
Psalm 112 Light shines in the darkness for the upright. (Ps. 112:4)
1 Corinthians 2:1-12

Having read these readings, consider this:

The Sermon on the Mount calls the Christian community to righteousness and, specifically, to being salt and light for the world. Thus, Christians together should so live as to help preserve life on the earth and to show a way that humans should go. The problem is that we are often like the people in Isaiah: wanting to be religious but hiding from the real suffering in the world. At the heart of our reading of these scriptures, however, and at the heart of our assembly, lives the hidden wisdom of God, poured out among us by the Spirit of God. That wisdom is Jesus Christ crucified. Christ is the true light of the world. His cross is its salt. Baptized into him, taught by him, and fed by him, we are given the Spirit. Then we may in humility begin again to meet the fierce requirements of this sermon: to share bread with the hungry, care for the homeless, act to repair the holes in the fabric of our common life. Such response, even if it is only a halting beginning, will be as light and salt and water for the world.

SIXTH SUNDAY AFTER EPIPHANY *(if before Transfiguration)* SUNDAY, FEBRUARY 11–17 LECTIONARY 6, PROPER 1

Matthew 5:21-37
Deuteronomy 30:15-20
Psalm 119:1-8 Happy are they who follow the teaching of the LORD. (Ps. 119:1)
1 Corinthians 3:1-9

Having read these readings, consider this:

According to Deuteronomy, when we consider the commandments of God, both blessings and curses—that is, both life and death—are set before us. But then, paying attention to Jesus, we are in significant trouble. In Matthew's Sermon on the Mount, Jesus intensifies the commandments, makes them harder, makes them deal not only with actions but with attitudes. None of us escapes this condemnation. "You will never get out," is our sentence from this judge. Jesus, who speaks these heightened commandments, is the very presence of God: "I say to you," he says as with the voice of God. But this Jesus is also the one who was utterly faithful, not divorcing us, the one who was murdered, and the one who in his resurrection is the yes to all of God's promises. The assembly where we gather is God's garden, God's building, and the gospel that plants and builds is the good news of this crucified and risen Jesus in the midst of this assembly. The Spirit poured out from God gives the growth. Turn to this assembly for hope and comfort. Hear the gospel. Enact the peace, being reconciled with others as the Sermon on the Mount proposes. Eat God's mercy in the holy meal. Then start again to show profound respect to each person you meet, to recover faithfulness in all your promises, and to say yes to God's life-giving intentions for us and the world.

SEVENTH SUNDAY AFTER EPIPHANY *(if before Transfiguration)*
SUNDAY, FEBRUARY 18–24
LECTIONARY 7, PROPER 2

Matthew 5:38-48
Leviticus 19:1-2, 9-18
Psalm 119:33-40 Teach me, O LORD, the way of your statutes. (Ps. 119:33)
1 Corinthians 3:10-11, 16-23

Having read these readings, consider this:

In Matthew, Jesus tells us to be perfect as God is perfect. In Leviticus, the holiness code tells us to be holy as God is holy. Is Paul also telling us to be the temple of God, the place where the world can encounter God? We cannot do it. Leviticus gives yet more content to these demands, especially calling us to justice and care for the poor, while Matthew's Jesus heightens the commands of Leviticus with beautiful but nearly impossible requirements. The texts accuse us. But Paul does not tell us to be the temple of God. He says that the assembly of Christians (the "you" is plural) together is the temple of God, the place where the Spirit dwells. The Spirit bears witness to the wise foolishness of the crucified and risen Christ, the one who does give to everyone who asks. We are the beggars. In this word and in the holy supper, he gives us forgiveness and mercy. Indeed, in Christ we are given all things. Then we turn again to our neighbors, learning from Jesus Christ to give, turn our cheek, share our clothing, go the extra mile, and pray for our enemies.

EIGHTH SUNDAY AFTER EPIPHANY *(if before Transfiguration)*
SUNDAY, FEBRUARY 25–MARCH 1
LECTIONARY 8, PROPER 3

Matthew 6:24-34
Isaiah 49:8-16a
Psalm 131 Like a child upon its mother's breast, my soul is quieted within me. (Ps. 131:2)
1 Corinthians 4:1-5

Having read these readings, consider this:

There is great comfort in these readings. Even if letting worry go is easier said than done, perhaps these images can hold us into a deeper peace: God is like a loving father who will provide for us food and drink and clothing just as the birds of the air and the lilies of the field are so cared for. God is like a loving mother who can never forget her nursing child. As the psalm sings, God is the mother who holds us into quiet rest. And even were such mothers and fathers to forget their children, God will not: we are written on God's hands. The hands on which we are inscribed are the wounded hands of Christ. Come to the assembly in him, walking past the spring of water that is baptism. Then see how, in the power of the Spirit, God clothes us with Christ and feeds us with mercy at the holy table. Let go of fear and worry. Let go of judging others as well. Do not judge even yourself. Christ, who gives forgiveness here, is the only reliable judge.

TRANSFIGURATION OF OUR LORD
LAST SUNDAY AFTER EPIPHANY

Matthew 17:1-9
Exodus 24:12-18
Psalm 2 You are my son; this day have I begotten you. (Ps. 2:7)
2 Peter 1:16-21

Having read these readings, consider this:

The story in Exodus says that after six days on the mountain, Moses encountered God's glory and entered the cloud for forty days to be given the law, the law to which the people will listen. Matthew says that after six days, Jesus and three disciples go up another mountain. But now Jesus is the shining one, the presence of God's glory, the one to whom we should listen. Moses and Elijah, who have both seen God on a mountain, bear witness to him. In Matthew this event takes place six days after Jesus has foretold his death. We come to understand that the crucified Christ is the very glorious one of whom we hear. Now we will enter Lent for forty days to go up to the full celebration of that death and resurrection. More: the dwelling that Peter wanted to make has been built here: it is the assembly where we hear the scriptures inspired by the Spirit of God; the place where we listen to the risen Christ and gather at his holy table; the gathering where Jesus tells us not to be afraid and where the morning star rises in our hearts. Illumined by the light of Christ shining in the assembly, we can turn to help also our neighbors be free from fear.

ASH WEDNESDAY

See above, in chapter 2.

FIRST SUNDAY IN LENT

Matthew 4:1-11
Genesis 2:15-17; 3:1-7
Psalm 32 Mercy embraces those who trust in the Lord. (Ps. 32:10)
Romans 5:12-19

Having read these readings, consider this:

We are ourselves the Adam and Eve of this true myth: we are often the ones who believe the lie that we can be like God; our supposed wisdom is often simply sadness and the knowledge that we are naked. But there is Another, the one from whom comes the free gift of life and grace for all, though he shares human hunger and mortality with us. The other story of this day, the story of his being tested by the devil, redoes the Genesis account and gives us hope. It also presents ahead of time the awful testing of his cross. In Matthew, the crowd derides him, saying, “If you are the Son of God, come down from the cross” (27:40). In the wilderness, Jesus answers with scriptural quotes from Deuteronomy. At the cross, where he has no bread, no angelic help, no power, and at last no life, he answers silently. Now Lent comes to be a way of healing for Adam and Eve, leading us like catechumens back to our baptism into Christ. In the assembly, by the power of the Spirit, God gives us the risen Christ as our bread, the scriptures Jesus quotes as our continued help in any test, and Jesus Christ himself as the only reliable king. Such mercy embraces us so that we may turn with real wisdom toward the needs of the world.

SECOND SUNDAY IN LENT

John 3:1-17
Genesis 12:1-4a
Psalm 121 I lift up my eyes to the hills; my help comes from the LORD. (Ps. 121:1, 2)
Romans 4:1-5, 13-17

Having read these readings, consider this:

We continue now to journey toward baptism and baptismal renewal at Easter, and we do so in this year A accompanied by great stories from the Old Testament and by the discourses and signs of John's gospel. Trusting God, Abraham goes out toward a promised new life that will give blessing to all the earth. Nicodemus the teacher is himself taught that such new life begins with a birth from water and the Spirit, what the church calls baptism. In baptism, we join Abraham in trusting that God makes something out of nothing, that through Christ, God gives life to the dead, and that in the Spirit God justifies the ungodly. These are lively and important ways of stating the three articles of the baptismal creed. Gathered into the reality of these promises, we are again sent to bear witness in our lives to how much God loves the world.

THIRD SUNDAY IN LENT

John 4:5-42
Exodus 17:1-7
Psalm 95 Let us shout for joy to the rock of our salvation. (Ps. 95:1)
Romans 5:1-11

Having read these readings, consider this:

We are all the woman of Samaria, thirsty for hope and life. Our baptism identifies us with all such thirsty people. By seeing ourselves together with her, we also see the meaning of our baptism into the living water given by Christ: by his gift, from the cross and today in worship, we and all the needy ones are given the reliable water to drink. He is the Rock from whom we slake our thirst. He is the source of the Spirit poured into our hearts. We too may tell the people in our village.

FOURTH SUNDAY IN LENT

John 9:1-41
1 Samuel 16:1-13
Psalm 23 You anoint my head with oil. (Ps. 23:5)
Ephesians 5:8-14

Having read these readings, consider this:

Here is yet another story of water. Two weeks ago, we heard in John 3 about being "born of water and the Spirit." Last Sunday, in John 4, Jesus offered us "living water." And today a man who has been blind all his life is made to see by a combination of the saliva from Jesus' body and the water of a pool called "Sent." Ancient Christians believed that all of these readings tell us of baptism. No matter how good or how poor our physical vision is, we are blind to the mercy of God, to the world the way God sees it, and to the needs of our neighbor. Fear can make us yet more blind. But Jesus is the one who is Sent; it is as if his cross and resurrection is a pool in which we can wash and once again see. He awakens us to light. He anoints us with the Spirit that enables us to walk without fear through the valley of the shadow of death. Then, baptized into his risen life, we are to turn and be something of the same gift to our neighbors, part of God's comfort to them, part of the goodness and mercy God makes to follow them.

FIFTH SUNDAY IN LENT

John 11:1-45
Ezekiel 37:1-14
Psalm 130 I wait for you, O LORD; in your word is my hope. (Ps. 130:5)
Romans 8:6-11

Having read these readings, consider this:

Christ comes to us in the scripture we have read. When he comes, he does to us now what he is doing in the text. We are the dry bones, especially in this difficult time. We are the dead and nearly dead. He calls us by name and says, "Come out." He tells those around us, "Unbind her and let her go; unbind him and let him go; unbind them and let them go." Because of baptism, the Spirit of God, the God who raised Jesus from the dead, dwells in us and makes us alive together with Christ. Then we should turn to those around us as best we can in this time and let them go.

SUNDAY OF THE PASSION, PALM SUNDAY

See above, in chapter 2.

THE THREE DAYS
MAUNDY THURSDAY, GOOD FRIDAY, VIGIL OF EASTER

See above, in chapter 2.

RESURRECTION OF OUR LORD, EASTER DAY

Matthew 28:1-10
Jeremiah 31:1-6
Psalm 118:1-2, 14-24 This is the day that the LORD has made; let us rejoice and be glad in it. (Ps. 118:24)
Colossians 3:1-4

Having read these readings, consider this:

This Easter we are indeed in the wilderness, and our life is indeed hidden. But because of the death and resurrection of Jesus Christ, we believe that the ancient promises to Israel are now extended to us. In the resurrection, God loves you with an everlasting love. God will again build you. Christ is your life and you shall appear with him. And today the Galilee, where by the power of the Spirit Jesus may be seen alive, is in our own assemblies. Against all sadness, "this is the day that the LORD has made; let us rejoice and be glad in it." Christ is risen! Alleluia!

SECOND SUNDAY OF EASTER

John 20:19-31
Acts 2:14a, 22-32
Psalm 16 In your presence there is fullness of joy. (Ps. 16:11)
1 Peter 1:3-9

Having read these readings, consider this:

It is a week later, and we are still mostly behind locked doors. We do not see, and at least sometimes, we certainly doubt. But these texts are full of blessing on those who do not see. The Gospel according to John is written so that, though we do not see the risen Christ, we may believe in him. The second reading says rightly that though we do not see him, we love him. And today, this very Sunday, Christ comes to us, wherever we are, bringing peace, forgiveness, and the Spirit of life and hope. Amazingly, we can reach out together to touch his body in the holy communion. And with our ears and eyes we touch Christ's wounds in the scripture itself. We are once again made witnesses to the resurrection for the sake of all our neighbors.

THIRD SUNDAY OF EASTER

Luke 24:13-35
Acts 2:14a, 36-41
Psalm 116:1-4, 12-29 I will call on the name of the LORD. (Ps. 116:13)
1 Peter 1:17-23

Having read these readings, consider this:

Psalm 116 speaks of the "cords of death" and the "anguish of the grave." It is as if all the world now is bound by such cords, held in such anguish. But the risen Christ opens to us the word of the scriptures. We recognize him there. We have been born anew by his word and have received the gift of the Holy Spirit by baptism in Christ's name. Then, with the disciples at Emmaus, we can see the risen Lord in the breaking of the bread of the holy communion, and we can go to others to tell them what we have seen. More: even were we not able to gather as church, even were the recent pandemic to return, the Risen One stays with us in our homes, speaks to us in the word of God, is present at our meals, and blesses us in our worst distresses. But the assembly around word and sacrament abides. In every future we will again "lift the cup of salvation" together as we did in the past. We will again run to tell others. The promise is for us all.

FOURTH SUNDAY OF EASTER

John 10:1-10
Acts 2:42-47
Psalm 23 The Lord is my shepherd; I shall not be in want. (Ps. 23:1)
1 Peter 2:19-25

Having read these readings, consider this:

There are lots of "thieves and robbers" about. That is, there are church leaders who do not present the gospel, and there are political leaders who serve only themselves. The Bible calls such leaders "false shepherds." But in the Bible the Good Shepherd, the one who gathers the flock and does not misuse or kill them, is God. In his death and resurrection, Jesus—who is called the Lamb of God—becomes our Good Shepherd. By his wounds we were healed. In the current valley of death, he is with us. In the scriptures, as in the preaching of faithful pastors and the witness of each other, we hear the voice of God the shepherd, calling us by name. In baptism the Spirit leads us beside still waters. In the supper, the Risen One prepares a table for us. And this holy Trinity turns us again toward people in need, toward people hurt by the thieves and robbers.

FIFTH SUNDAY OF EASTER

John 14:1-14
Acts 7:55-60
Psalm 31:1-5, 15-16 Into your hands, O Lord, I commend my spirit. (Ps. 31:5)
1 Peter 2:2-10

Having read these readings, consider this:

Thomas knows neither the way nor where Jesus is going. Philip wants to see God. These disciples stand for us, now, in our need and confusion. But Jesus himself is the way, the truth, and the life. He is himself the presence of God. The amazing thing is that he goes to God now by going to the cross, and he makes that place of suffering to be the very dwelling place of God with us. Henceforth, in every place of suffering, we see the risen Christ already there, as Stephen sees him coming. In Jesus, God has mercy on us and makes us together the house of God and the witnesses to God's mighty acts. In the Spirit, Jesus' words come to us in assembly—and in our own homes—and make our assemblies and our homes to be part of this house of God with many rooms. From this house we can turn to our neighbors with our prayers and gifts, for God's mercy is for all.

SIXTH SUNDAY OF EASTER

John 14:15-21
Acts 17:22-31
Psalm 66:8-20 Bless our God, you peoples; let the sound of praise be heard. (Ps. 66:8)
1 Peter 3:13-22

Having read these readings, consider this:

Our religion and our religious practice must not be a monument to an unknown God. We do indeed live within the boundaries of our mortality and the limits of our knowledge. We know that we die. And right now we certainly do not know enough about the future. But we are not left simply to grope for God. Rather, within those boundaries Christ comes to us, making us alive together with him. In him we know God and that God is not far from any one of us. Christ has died to bring us to God. In our baptism Christ has made us a family, even if we are distant from each other. The Spirit poured out from his resurrection abides with us, binding us together. We see the living Christ in the word, a place of refreshment for us, and in the holy meal. Both word and sacrament bid us not to fear, but gently and reverently to tell our world and our neighbors about the hope that is in us.

ASCENSION OF OUR LORD, THE FORTIETH DAY OF EASTER

See above, in chapter 2.

SEVENTH SUNDAY OF EASTER

John 17:1-11
Acts 1:6-14
Psalm 68:1-10, 32-35 Sing to God, who rides upon the clouds. (Ps. 68:4)
1 Peter 4:12-14; 5:6-11

Having read these readings, consider this:

Our brothers and sisters in all the world are indeed undergoing suffering now. Amid that suffering, there are sometimes too many words: complaints, misinformation, self-justifications, accusations. But Jesus Christ has given us the very words of God. And those words will restore, support, strengthen, and establish us. They give us life. They will make us one with God and so with all of God's people. Usually, the church hears those words of God in the words of forgiveness at the font, in the scriptures read and preached in the assembly, and in the very body and blood of Christ given to us together to eat and drink. And amazingly, whether we are together or alone, the very words of God are still given to us: we read and sing them in the assembly like those early Christians devoted to prayer in that Jerusalem house; we read and sing them in our homes, echoing that assembly. Here are three of the words we have now: "Resist the roaring lion" who wants to devour you with anger and fear. And "cast all your anxiety on God, for God cares for you." And "love one another as I have loved you."

DAY OF PENTECOST, THE FIFTIETH DAY OF EASTER

John 20:19-23
Acts 2:1-21
Psalm 104:24-34, 35b Send forth your Spirit and renew the face of the earth. (Ps. 104:30)
1 Corinthians 12:3b-13

Having read these readings, consider this:

There are certainly spirits abroad in the world and even in our own lives that do not work for the common good. There are certainly people—and perhaps we have been among them—who think that only their own language and culture can speak the truth and that people unlike them cannot have visions of hope that matter: "They are just drunk." But this attitude does not mark the Spirit of God, the Spirit given us when we are drawn into the word of God and into faithful prayer. God's Spirit comes from and bears witness to the risen Christ. It enables forgiveness—God's forgiveness of us, our forgiveness of each other, and our ministry of forgiveness to all the world. That Spirit gives us all differing abilities to use for building each other up. It gives vision and wisdom for all. In our baptism into Christ, God's Spirit has formed us into one body, and that body is quite alive in our assemblies and in the ministries to which we are sent in the world. Now we are to bear witness to our neighbors and greet the world with Christ's peace.

THE HOLY TRINITY
FIRST SUNDAY AFTER PENTECOST

Matthew 28:16-20
Genesis 1:1—2:4a
Psalm 8 How majestic is your name in all the earth! (Ps. 8:1)
2 Corinthians 13:11-13

Having read these readings, consider this:

There are lots of ideas around the world about who God is. Not all of them are life-giving. And there are lots of temptations right now to forget about any God and to live only for ourselves. These texts call us again to faith in the Holy One who is also the Holy Three; the God who surrounds us with grace, love, and communion; the God who made and holds the world; the God who—against all grief and sorrow—still calls the creation "very good." Baptized into the powerful name of this God and assured of the presence of the risen Christ, we greet each other with the peace and love that bear witness to this God. We know that God's beloved world now is in great need of that ordered peace and love.

SUNDAY, MAY 24–28 *(if after Holy Trinity)*
LECTIONARY 8, PROPER 3

See above, at Eighth Sunday after Epiphany, February 25–March 1.

SUNDAY, MAY 29–JUNE 4 *(if after Holy Trinity)*
LECTIONARY 9, PROPER 4

Matthew 7:21-29
Deuteronomy 11:18-21, 26-28
Psalm 31:1-5, 19-24 Be my strong rock, a castle to keep me safe. (Ps. 31:3)
Romans 1:16-17; 3:22b-28

Having read these readings, consider this:

Our houses—the "house" of our life or the "house" of our church assemblies—can fall if they are built on a bad foundation. Just doing religious deeds is not enough. But then what is the word on which to build? What is the word to put in our hearts and bind on all the occasions of our life? There is some tension between Matthew and Paul in answering that question. Luther, who found the summary of the gospel revealed in Romans 3:28, counsels us to start with Paul. All of us have sinned, and God's forgiving and justifying grace is given to us all in Jesus Christ. The Spirit awakens us to trust in that grace and so to live. The word and sacraments of our assemblies are rightly full of that grace. Build on that grace. Lie down and rise in that grace. Teach that grace to your children. Go out of your doors to the world with that grace. Then, with the rock of Christ as foundation, let all the words of the Sermon on the Mount, which comes to a conclusion this Sunday, challenge us again and again as we turn to the needs of our needy world.

SUNDAY, JUNE 5–11 *(if after Holy Trinity)*
LECTIONARY 10, PROPER 5

Matthew 9:9-13, 18-26
Hosea 5:15—6:6
Psalm 50:7-15 Call upon me in the day of trouble, says your God. (Ps. 50:15)
Romans 4:13-25

Having read these readings, consider this:

The church is a hospital for sinners and for those wounded by life, and these texts are full of healing. Matthew combines the story of Jesus eating with tax collectors with a simplified version of the Markan story of Jesus healing a bleeding woman and a dead girl. Hosea provides the original text that Jesus quotes while giving a marvelous account of the healing God. And Paul describes the faith of Abraham. We are addressed by all three texts: In the assembly, we are at table with Jesus, receiving forgiveness and mercy. He is that mercy. Even if we have been killed by the severe word of God, we are raised to life with the woman and the daughter of the synagogue ruler. And just as Abraham trusted God though he was "as good as dead," we are brought by the Spirit to have faith in the one who raised Jesus from the dead. Thus the holy Trinity heals us. These texts together are like spring rains, and together they show what it means to "know the Lord." Learning that mercy, we also learn to show mercy to others.

SUNDAY, JUNE 12–18 *(if after Holy Trinity)*
LECTIONARY 11, PROPER 6

Matthew 9:35—10:8
Exodus 19:2-8a
Psalm 100 We are God's people and the sheep of God's pasture. (Ps. 100:3)
Romans 5:1-8

Having read these readings, consider this:

Surely we, as well as our neighbors, are among the harassed and helpless whom Jesus sees, those with "every disease and every sickness." But as the baptized, we are also those to whom Jesus has committed his mission, and we have often failed. Nonetheless, God says, "I have brought you to myself." Because of Jesus Christ and in his word and sacrament, forgiveness and love have been poured into our hearts through the Holy Spirit. Just as the Twelve stand for the Israelites, called to be a people of priests for all the world, we too are given the charge to pray for all and to bear witness to the healing love of God, all of us together Christ's priestly people for the sake of the world.

SUNDAY, JUNE 19–25 *(if after Holy Trinity)*
LECTIONARY 12, PROPER 7

Matthew 10:24-39
Jeremiah 20:7-13
Psalm 69:7-18 Answer me, O Lord, for your love is kind. (Ps. 69:16)
Romans 6:1b-11

Having read these readings, consider this:

There is terror all around. Violence and destruction, too. Telling the truth about that condition of the world, however, has always been unpopular. Jeremiah experienced rejection. Even more, Jesus was killed. And Jesus calls us to follow him, to be countercultural like Jeremiah, to value the gospel of Jesus Christ even more than what the world counts as "family values," to tell the truth openly about human sin and God's mercy. It will not be easy. Still, because of Jesus' death and resurrection and our baptism into him, we can live a new life, unafraid of death. We can trust that we are seen and cared for, even in this time, as surely as God sees the sparrow. And we can tell others of this care, by our words and by our lives.

SUNDAY, JUNE 26–JULY 2
LECTIONARY 13, PROPER 8

Matthew 10:40-42
Jeremiah 28:5-9
Psalm 89:1-4, 15-18 Your love, O LORD, forever will I sing. (Ps. 89:1)
Romans 6:12-23

Having read these readings, consider this:

"War, famine, and pestilence," prophesied by the ancient prophets, are all around us today. We may wish to listen to people who speak of peace instead. We may long to say "amen" to their promises. But false comfort is worse than no comfort at all. Instead, in a hard time, we who have been baptized into Christ should offer welcome to people who speak the truth, and we should offer comfort—"a cup of cold water"—to the least and littlest ones, the ones hurt by these times. The truth-speakers are the very emissaries of the Holy Spirit. And the little ones, the vulnerable and unjustly treated ones, are the very presence of Jesus Christ to us. The truth in Christ saves us, turning our bodies from sin to real righteousness, from death to real life, from lies to love. Such life comes as the free gift of God in Jesus Christ.

SUNDAY, JULY 3–9
LECTIONARY 14, PROPER 9

Matthew 11:16-19, 25-30
Zechariah 9:9-12
Psalm 145:8-14 The LORD is gracious and full of compassion. (Ps. 145:8)
Romans 7:15-25a

Having read these readings, consider this:

There are images for our times and an image for us in the first two readings today. "War horses," "battle bows," and "waterless pits for prisoners" may be archaic, but they can stand for the very real, violent conflict in our world today and for our own sense of imprisonment. And with Paul, we too are not able to do the good we wish we could do. Who will deliver us? Thanks be to God, indeed, through Jesus Christ our Lord. For us, Jesus is the humble one who by the cross brings hope, release, and peace. Jesus welcomes us sinners. Even if we are not wise, Jesus shows us who God is, bringing our whole assembly to stand in Christ before the Father. And Jesus gives us rest. By the power of the Spirit, baptism into Christ draws us into learning from him and carrying his yoke: we, too, will seek to live out of peace and give rest to our neighbors.

SUNDAY, JULY 10–16
LECTIONARY 15, PROPER 10

Matthew 13:1-9, 18-23
Isaiah 55:10-13
Psalm 65:9-13 Your paths overflow with plenty. (Ps. 65:11)
Romans 8:1-11

Having read these readings, consider this:

First, simply listen to the parable itself (vv. 1-9): the dominion of God is like someone sowing seed in a very hard place, a place impossible for growing, full of death. Yet, against all expectation, astonishing growth takes place, yielding a great harvest. That image gives us a way to talk about Jesus' death and resurrection and its meaning for us. We live in a hard place and a hard time. And we ourselves are full of death. Jesus shares our death, yet he becomes the source and beginning of the great harvest. Now the Spirit of the One who raised Jesus from the dead comes down on us like rain. We and all the earth are being made to live and sing. Then, second, use the explanation (vv. 18-23) to join the parable yourself: receive the life-giving word like the good soil; listen to the word of God, the gospel; receive Christ in the holy supper; and bear a harvest of love for your neighbor. The very trees will clap their hands.

SUNDAY JULY 17–23
LECTIONARY 16, PROPER 11

Matthew 13:24-30, 36-43
Isaiah 44:6-8
Psalm 86:11-17 Teach me your way, O Lord, and I will walk in your truth. (Ps. 86:11)
Romans 8:12-25

Having read these readings, consider this:

We certainly know groaning right now. Indeed, in these difficult times the whole creation seems to be groaning. And amid signs of awful division between people in our land, we are tempted to try to weed the field ourselves, to try to tear out and eliminate whoever we think is a "weed." But the parable warns us that we would be torn apart ourselves; we all are both wheat and weed. Rather, as Isaiah says, only God is the judge, and we are to be witnesses to God's patience and mercy. Furthermore, Paul invites us to hope. Our groaning prayer is the very Spirit of God in us, forming us to trust God as a dear father, bearing witness in us that because of Christ we are children of

God. In our Sunday assembly's intercessions and in our private prayers, we groan for the world together with Jesus in the garden and on the cross. Then, in his resurrection, Christ makes us to be pure wheat. In God's great harvest we are fed by the Bread of God and can be made into bread for our neighbor.

SUNDAY, JULY 24–30
LECTIONARY 17, PROPER 12

Matthew 13:31-33, 44-52
1 Kings 3:5-12
Psalm 119:129-136 When your word is opened, it gives light and understanding. (Ps. 119:130)
Romans 8:26-39

Having read these readings, consider this:

It is not only that we do not know how to pray as we ought in our hard times. And it is not only that we do not have enough wisdom for the challenges we are facing. It is also, if we speak of the actual situation of our current world, that we are genuinely "being killed all day long" by "hardship or distress or peril" and certainly by disease. But there is light and wisdom and life in the word we read today. Jesus Christ himself is the finder of the treasure and the pearl, and he gives these away to us. His despised cross, his death with us, is the "bush" that becomes a tree in which we may shelter. The risen presence in word and sacrament of this Crucified One is like the bread of the woman, enough for a multitude and life-giving—though usual religion, worried about both leaven and the cross, would call it unclean. Such is the surprising dominion of God. Nothing can separate us from this love, even if we do not understand it. And the Spirit helps us in our weakness to pray for our needy world in this time and to pray that our leaders might have something like Solomon's wisdom.

SUNDAY, JULY 31–AUGUST 6
LECTIONARY 18, PROPER 13

Matthew 14:13-21
Isaiah 55:1-5
Psalm 145:8-9, 14-21 You open wide your hand and satisfy the desire of every living thing. (Ps. 145:16)
Romans 9:1-5

Having read these readings, consider this:

The primary biblical symbol of the mercy of God is food. In the exodus story, God sustains the people with manna and water from the rock. In the Psalms, God is praised in this way: "You open wide your hand and satisfy the desire of every living thing." And when the people were in trouble, the prophet Isaiah gave the promise of water, wine, milk, and bread, without price: hunger and thirst, both really and metaphorically, have an answer in God. These stories are part of the stunning inheritance of the Jews, the covenants of mercy, of which Paul speaks. But because of the compassion of Jesus Christ, we people of the nations, we people who are right now deeply hungry for hope, are ourselves grafted into the promise of these stories. They are also for us. Turn to God with your hunger for hope. And then, empowered by our bread-giving Lord, we are together turned to the needy world around us: "You give them something to eat."

SUNDAY, AUGUST 7–13
LECTIONARY 19, PROPER 14

Matthew 14:22-33
1 Kings 19:9-18
Psalm 85:8-13 I will listen to what the Lord God is saying. (Ps. 85:8)
Romans 10:5-15

Having read these readings, consider this:

In the story, Elijah is in trouble, threatened with death. Peter is in trouble too, drowning in the chaos of the sea. Let the stories reflect our times. We and all our world also know the threat of death and chaos. But then, listen. God comes to Elijah not in wind, earthquake, or fire, but in the sound of sheer silence and in a voice that gives him a mission. Those sounds may be little in the world, but they are the very presence of God. And Jesus comes to the storm-tossed disciples with a word of comfort, "Here I AM; do not be afraid." He comes as the very presence of God, the one named "I AM" in the scriptures. As Paul says, this life-giving word from God is not far away but here, now, in our assembly around the good news, on our lips and in our hearts. With the psalmist, let us say, "I will listen to what the LORD God is saying." God in Christ is speaking peace to us right now. Then let us undertake the mission to speak that peace also to our neighbors.

SUNDAY, AUGUST 14–20
LECTIONARY 20, PROPER 15

Matthew 15:21-28
Isaiah 56:1, 6-8
Psalm 67 Let all the people praise you, O God. (Ps. 67:3)
Romans 11:1-2a, 29-32

Having read these readings, consider this:

If we tell the truth, we all are among the disobedient, as Paul so clearly says. We also are rightly among the foreigners, standing with the outsider woman, begging for help. We too are the dogs, with no right to the bread. But God holds all together in mercy, the ancient covenant people of the Jews but also those of us from the many peoples who have been gathered by the Lord. From Isaiah, from Paul, and from the Gospel according to Matthew, Christians have been learning the humility of the woman: "Yes, Lord, yet even the dogs eat the crumbs." Because of his cross and resurrection, Jesus Christ makes bread available to all the peoples, including us—the bread of the eucharist when we can gather, but always the bread of his healing word. And so we come to see our neighbor in a stunning new way: another needy person beside us, under God's mercy.

SUNDAY, AUGUST 21–27
LECTIONARY 21, PROPER 16

Matthew 16:13-20
Isaiah 51:1-6
Psalm 138 O LORD, your steadfast love endures forever. (Ps. 138:8)
Romans 12:1-8

Having read these readings, consider this:

If we think with sober judgment, as Paul counsels, we are none of us reliable as a rock. But then neither was Abraham, "the rock from which" the people of God "were hewn." Abraham believed God, but according to the stories, he also repeatedly lied. And to call Peter "the Rock"—Peter, who doubted and then denied Jesus—seems like a joke. But in Matthew, Jesus speaks blessing, mercy, and forgiveness to Peter. He speaks these also to us, in these scriptures and in the holy supper. Following Jesus, in our conversations with and prayers for each other and in our assembly greetings of peace, we can use the very keys that Peter is given, forgiving and loosing one another with the actual mercy of God, the mercy that will yet make of the afflicted earth a garden of thanksgiving. The forgiving mercy of God in the crucified Christ is the rock on which the church is built, even when all else falls and dies; it is the ground from which we turn in generosity to our needy neighbors, worshiping God by how we use our bodily lives.

SUNDAY, AUGUST 28–SEPTEMBER 3
LECTIONARY 22, PROPER 17

Matthew 16:21-28
Jeremiah 15:15-21
Psalm 26:1-8 Your love is before my eyes; I have walked faithfully with you. (Ps. 26:3)
Romans 12:9-21

Having read these readings, consider this:

We would often like to think that having faith in God should lead to an easy life. Jeremiah discovered the opposite. And in Matthew's gospel, Peter made a God-given confession last Sunday, but this Sunday he opposes Jesus by arguing for that easy life. Still, what is it to "take up our cross"? This is not a call to invent new sufferings nor to think we will save ourselves nor to counsel other people to put up with injustice. Rather, we need to tell the truth about how the world is full of suffering and see that in sharing our sufferings and death, God in Christ saves us all and shows us a way to follow behind him. Paul gives detail to that way: taking no vengeance, associating with people who are considered lowly, weeping with those who weep, not claiming to be wiser than we are, persevering in prayer, rejoicing in hope—those are some of the traits of the way of the cross for us. In the assembly we are strengthened for this humble way by receiving the gift of Christ's life-giving cross in the holy communion. At all times, we can gladly join Jeremiah in eating—trusting and taking deeply into our lives—the words we read.

SUNDAY, SEPTEMBER 4–10
LECTIONARY 23, PROPER 18

Matthew 18:15-20
Ezekiel 33:7-11
Psalm 119:33-40 I desire the path of your commandments. (Ps. 119:35)
Romans 13:8-14

Having read these readings, consider this:

Let Ezekiel the prophet speak to us today, in the name of God. If we do not turn from our own sins toward the mercy of God, we will waste away and die. And we are such sinners. But in Matthew, Jesus gives us a way of mutual forgiveness. The "keys" that he gave to Peter two Sundays ago he gives now to the whole church. When someone has offended us, we should not respond with gossip nor with announcing a grievance on social media, but with direct contact and mutual reconciliation. In the midst of our common life, especially as we are gathered in the assembly for prayer, the risen Christ dwells, as he promised. He is the source of all forgiveness, the ground of reconciliation. He dawns for us like the day. Baptized in his Spirit, we may put on Christ like clothing, which is to say: we may put on love for our neighbor.

SUNDAY, SEPTEMBER 11–17
LECTIONARY 24, PROPER 19

Matthew 18:21-35
Genesis 50:15-21
Psalm 103:1-13 LORD, you are full of compassion and mercy. (Ps. 103:8)
Romans 14:1-12

Having read these readings, consider this:

The readings accuse us: Like Joseph's brothers, we are afraid of people we have betrayed. Like Paul's readers, we often argue with each other about issues that do not matter. Like Peter in Matthew, we want to limit our forgiveness of others. But one who is greater than Joseph is here. Jesus Christ was thrown into a deeper pit than Joseph when he was taken to the cross. Yet in the resurrection he has become an even greater source of forgiveness and bread. Like the fictional king of the parable, God in Christ has forgiven us—each one of us—an impossible debt: 100,000 talents being something like 150,000 years of salary for a skilled worker. Strengthened by that forgiveness poured over us today by the Spirit alive in this word and in the bread and cup of Christ's gift, we are enabled again and again to forgive our neighbor whose debt to us, by comparison, is like only a few weeks of salary. Renewed in this mercy, we will live and die to the Lord Jesus, giving praise to God.

SUNDAY, SEPTEMBER 18–24
LECTIONARY 25, PROPER 20

Matthew 20:1-16
Jonah 3:10—4:11
Psalm 145:1-8 The LORD is slow to anger and abounding in steadfast love. (Ps. 145:8)
Philippians 1:21-30

Having read these readings, consider this:

The old story goes that Jonah does not want Israel's ancient enemies forgiven, for he does not think they deserve it. Then in Matthew's parable, the first workers, expecting that they themselves should get more, do not think the latecomers deserve full pay. Do we draw lines about who is deserving and who not? The gospel is ever teaching us that if we draw a line to exclude someone, Jesus Christ is always on the other side of the line: in the cross he is with the unsalaried, the suffering poor, the sinners, the enemies, even the threatened animals. And he is risen to give away mercy to all, to give enough to live this day. The justice and "fairness" of God is mercy. And none of us is deserving. We, too, are latecomers—beggars for life—and God's gift is for us all, without distinction. Such mercy gives us an utterly new way to see the world and an invitation to live our life in a manner worthy of the gospel.

SUNDAY, SEPTEMBER 25–OCTOBER 1
LECTIONARY 26, PROPER 21

Matthew 21:23-32
Ezekiel 18:1-4, 25-32
Psalm 25:1-9 Remember, O Lord, your compassion and love. (Ps. 25:6)
Philippians 2:1-13

Having read these readings, consider this:

Though the ten commandments say that punishment for the iniquity of parents will go on to the third and fourth generation, the prophet Ezekiel says otherwise: we shall be punished for only our own sins. Then the prophet counsels us to get a new heart. This prophetic word is still very hard: our own sins are more than enough for serious punishment; like the sons in the parable, we are often the ones who boldly say yes to the will of God and then do nothing. And how shall we get a new heart? But the Gospel according to Matthew has begun to turn toward the story of the cross, and in this Sunday's narrative Jesus stands in the temple, mysterious in his authority, warning the world's authorities and showing mercy to outsiders and sinners. Paul shows us where that mystery goes: through Christ's death and resurrection, present in word and sacrament, God is at work in us. For a new heart, we are together given the mind of Christ. There is indeed much consolation, compassion, and sharing of the Spirit in this word. Starting again, in humility, we may look to the needs of others in a profoundly needy world.

SUNDAY, OCTOBER 2–8
LECTIONARY 27, PROPER 22

Matthew 21:33-46
Isaiah 5:1-7
Psalm 80:7-15 Look down from heaven, O God; behold and tend this vine. (Ps. 80:14, 15)
Philippians 3:4b-14

Having read these readings, consider this:

Here is an old biblical allegory: Israel is a vineyard from which God, as the vineyard owner, expects to see the good wine of justice and righteousness produced. That image is present in two of our readings as well as the psalm today. We would misuse this allegory, however, if we made it anti-Semitic, as too many Christians have done. We ourselves are now the tenants of that vineyard. We are the ones who have contributed to injustice, to the weeping of the misused, even to bloodshed. The son has died because of us. Still, these texts really are a love-song. We are accused because God loves us, wishing to turn us to hear the gospel. For us, Christ is the rejected stone that has become the cornerstone. In mercy, Christ Jesus has made us his own. In the Spirit, he gives us the good wine of himself. Then, in the power of the resurrection and even by sharing his sufferings, we may begin again to do justice for our neighbors in this needy world.

SUNDAY, OCTOBER 9–15
LECTIONARY 28, PROPER 23

Matthew 22:1-14
Isaiah 25:1-9
Psalm 23 You prepare a table before me, and my cup is running over. (Ps. 23:5)
Philippians 4:1-9

Having read these readings, consider this:

This is a hard time for us to think about whatever is true, honorable, just, commendable . . . So much violence, sickness, death, and divisiveness surround us. The ancient image of the banquet at the end of time, the feast to which all peoples are invited and at which death is finally destroyed, sounds wonderful. But where is it? We may rightly feel more like the unprepared guest who has been thrown out. But the promise of God is sure. The Lord is indeed near. In his cross and resurrection, Jesus Christ has himself swallowed death, and even now he is our shepherd, preparing the table before us, wiping tears away from all faces, being the refuge of the poor. We may come to the feast in church. And in the assembly, as also at home, we may, in the power of the Spirit, feast on the word, clothed with the garment of God's mercy right now. Then, rejoicing in the Lord and adopting God's own gentleness, we may join in the wiping away of tears on the faces of others.

SUNDAY, OCTOBER 16–22
LECTIONARY 29, PROPER 24

Matthew 22:15-22
Isaiah 45:1-7
Psalm 96 Ascribe to the Lord honor and power. (Ps. 96:7)
1 Thessalonians 1:1-10

Having read these readings, consider this:

In this account, found in all three synoptic gospels, Jesus says we should pay our taxes. Only, for us there is no Caesar. Our commitment is to functioning government, to government "by the people." When we are the government, we should gladly pay our taxes, but even more, we should give what belongs to our shared government by voting. And we should endeavor to see that the taxes are spent justly, especially to aid the most vulnerable, like Cyrus letting the captive people go. All of that is what Luther would call God's "left hand," in which God mysteriously governs the world through the powers that be. But what about God's "right hand"? Jesus Christ, the one who is being threatened with arrest and death in this story, is himself the very image of God. He is our head. His cross finally holds together and inscribes all things. Everything is God's, not only the government. By the power of the Spirit, Jesus gives life and salvation to us in his word and in his supper, so that, like Paul and the Thessalonians, we can receive this word with joy and, in turn, give thanks for, pray for, and give support to the earth and our neighbor. That is giving to God what is God's.

SUNDAY, OCTOBER 23–29
LECTIONARY 30, PROPER 25

Matthew 22:34-46
Leviticus 19:1-2, 15-18
Psalm 1 Their delight is in the law of the Lord. (Ps. 1:2)
1 Thessalonians 2:1-8

Having read these readings, consider this:

Two principles mark the Christian way to read the Bible: First, loving God and neighbor is all the law. And second, the crucified Jesus Christ is Lord. But here is the deep truth, a truth we rightly repeat to our shame: "We have not loved our neighbor as ourselves." What shall we do? Where do we turn? In the crucified and risen Jesus Christ we meet the very Lord who is holy, and here is his holiness: even more than Paul who was his follower, this Jesus shares with us his very own self, doing so in the word and in the supper. Forgiven by this gospel of God, we are made free in the Spirit to turn in love to our neighbor again. Since this Sunday may occur near to Reformation Day, we rightly remember that such a reading of the Bible is close to the heart of any commemoration of that day.

SUNDAY, OCTOBER 30–NOVEMBER 5
LECTIONARY 31, PROPER 26

Matthew 23:1-12
Micah 3:5-12
Psalm 43 Send out your light and truth, that they may lead me. (Ps. 43:3)
1 Thessalonians 2:9-13

Having read these readings, consider this:

These readings ought not be used for anti-Semitism. Rather, they speak to us now, declaring our transgression: We are too often those who practice religion in order to be noticed and praised. We sometimes push a religious practice onto other people that is hard for them to bear. Among us are also religious leaders who insist on elevated titles, yet who give good news only to those who pay for it. As in Micah, the ruin of our cities may well be our lot. But the Humble One, the one who went to the cross and gives himself in the holy supper, stands as our true instructor. The Spirit poured out from him has formed and still forms all the saints to serve. And the one he called "Father" is our God. We are gathered by that holy Trinity. As Paul spoke the gospel powerfully but without burdening his hearers, so we too gather in assembly around the grace-filled word of this God. That word at work in us can bring us again and again to do justice for our neighbor.

ALL SAINTS DAY (NOVEMBER 1) OR ALL SAINTS SUNDAY

Matthew 5:1-12
Revelation 7:9-17
Psalm 34:1-10, 22 Fear the LORD, you saints of the LORD; for those who fear the LORD lack nothing. (Ps. 34:9)
1 John 3:1-3

Having read these readings, consider this:

We can hardly avoid knowing, in these days, that we are surrounded by so much death: those hurt by epidemics, those killed by the violence of terrorism and war, our own beloved dead. And we ourselves are often afraid. All Saints Day comes with these texts this year to speak life and comfort. With all the children of God; with all the baptized, living and dead; with our own congregation; with all the unknown and unheralded ones who in making peace and showing mercy bore witness to God—with all of them we sing to God and to the Lamb. That Lamb, Jesus Christ, is himself the most profound example of all the values praised in the beatitudes. We are washed and saved in his blood. Now we will undertake again to live in the Spirit of those values: joy, mercy, simplicity. And usually at about this time, in civic responsibility, we will pray to elect public officials who themselves manifest something of that Spirit.

SUNDAY, NOVEMBER 6–12
LECTIONARY 32, PROPER 27

Matthew 25:1-13
Amos 5:18-24
Psalm 70 You are my helper and my deliverer; O Lord, do not tarry. (Ps. 70:5)
1 Thessalonians 4:13-18

Having read these readings, consider this:

As the darkness around us grows and the vegetation dies, Christians turn to think of the end of our lives and the end of time. All three readings today join in that thinking. Amos warns us not to imagine that the day of the Lord will be wonderful for us unless we have done justice to our neighbors. Matthew warns us to stay awake; without wisdom we could be excluded in the end. But Paul uses old cosmological imagery to assure us that the death and resurrection of Christ brings life to all, the living and the dead. In fact, for Christians, the wedding feast has already begun. Though we have often slept, Jesus Christ has stayed awake for us and has shared with us his oil. In Christ's death and resurrection God's marriage with the earth has begun. As we gather in assembly for the feast now, the Holy Spirit kindles for us the lamp of the word. By the light of that word let us begin again to do justice in a needy world. And in this election season, no matter who has been elected, as concerned citizens let us call for them to do justice as well.

SUNDAY, NOVEMBER 13–19
LECTIONARY 33, PROPER 28

Matthew 25:14-30
Zephaniah 1:7, 12-18
Psalm 90:1-12 So teach us to number our days that we may apply our hearts to wisdom. (Ps. 90:12)
1 Thessalonians 5:1-11

Having read these readings, consider this:

Here at the end of the church year and at the end of Matthew, the readings from the Bible are as harsh as they ever get. But much in our world seems to fit these pictures. When we fail to act in justice and to use for the common good what God has entrusted to us, a day of darkness and gloom—Matthew's "outer darkness"—descends upon us. We rightly pray, as Jesus taught us, "Save us from the time of trial, and deliver us from evil." And God does save us. The good news this Sunday is in the second reading: in Jesus Christ, God has made salvation and not wrath to be our future. By the power of the Spirit poured out from the risen Christ, we have been clothed in faith and love and hope, like armor in dangerous times. The word of God awakens us to live as if in a light-filled day, even when surrounded by the experience of difficulty and evil. And amazingly, Paul also says that whether we are awake or asleep, Christ has shared our death that we may live with him. In gratitude, we have a chance again to use what we have been given for the well-being of our neighbor.

CHRIST THE KING
SUNDAY, NOVEMBER 20–26
LECTIONARY 34, PROPER 29

Matthew 25:31-46
Ezekiel 34:11-16, 20-24
Psalm 95:1-7a We are the people of God's pasture and the sheep of God's hand. (Ps. 95:7)
Ephesians 1:15-23

Having read these readings, consider this:

The parable judges us: we have certainly not always given food and drink to the hungry and thirsty, nor welcome to the stranger, nor help to the naked, sick, and imprisoned. But God is also full of mercy. Indeed, this Sunday comes to show us who this God really is: the one whom Jesus calls "Father," who passionately cares for the world and gathers the scattered and injured of the people—including us—judging all rulers who misuse the weak; the one true shepherd, Jesus Christ, who in his cross identifies with all the wretched poor and remains as close to us as the closest needy person; and the Spirit who gives us wisdom to know this one God and who mercifully makes of us a community—the assembly of the church—to bear witness in the world. This Sunday of the last judgment is also a kind of Trinity Sunday, a revelation of the one God who fills all in all. Such good news comes to us in the word and in the eucharist, like food for a hungry flock, turning us again away from fear to care for our needy neighbor, helping us to be more "sheep" than "goats."

CHAPTER 4

Readings for Year B

FIRST SUNDAY OF ADVENT

Mark 13:24-37
Isaiah 64:1-9
Psalm 80:1-7, 17-19 Let your face shine upon us, and we shall be saved. (Ps. 80:7)
1 Corinthians 1:3-9

Having read these readings, consider this:

Isaiah gives us words for the longings that are present in all the world: "O that you, O God, would tear open the heavens and come down!" We are rightly afraid that our sins have delayed and hidden God's coming to us with healing and hope. We know ourselves to be held by our iniquity rather than held by God the merciful potter. But in Mark's gospel, Jesus joins us in not knowing when the day of healing will be. And in the very next chapter, the gospel begins to tell of his death. We are to keep awake, like a doorkeeper watching for the return of the homeowner. Then the amazing thing happens—God does come: at evening, in the supper when Jesus gives himself away and prays in the garden; at midnight, when he is arrested; at cockcrow, when he is denied; at dawn, when he begins to be taken to the cross; and yet again at dawn, when the women at the door of the tomb discover that he is risen. In Mark's gospel the heavens have been torn open and God has come among all the world's suffering. Christ is with us still. Forgiven and strengthened by this word, as

Paul says, as also by the continuing presence of Christ in his supper, we may wait for his full revealing. We are called to be doorkeepers still watching on behalf of all the needy world and yet bearing witness to God's present mercy.

SECOND SUNDAY OF ADVENT

Mark 1:1-8
Isaiah 40:1-11
Psalm 85:1-2, 8-13 Righteousness shall prepare a pathway for God. (Ps. 85:13)
2 Peter 3:8-15a

Having read these readings, consider this:

We are indeed like grass. And we rightly join the crowd coming to John, confessing our sins. So we wait for the day of God, the day when the more powerful one comes, when the shepherd God gently leads the hurt exiles home, when all the earth and sky will be made new, when righteousness and peace will kiss each other. We wait. When will that day come? The Gospel of Mark itself is waiting: the book is named "the beginning of the good news." When will we receive the good news itself? Now. Here. The whole gospel book shows us the crucified and risen Jesus Christ who is to be seen now among us, especially when we are able to assemble, when we remember how Christ has baptized us together in the Holy Spirit. But Christ is also seen among all the little, needy, waiting ones of the world. He is the powerful one hidden in our waiting world, God with us in the withering grass. The healing has begun. Jesus Christ by the poured-out Spirit makes of us, even in hard times, heralds to say to our cities—to say with our words and our deeds—"Here is your God."

THIRD SUNDAY OF ADVENT

John 1:6-8, 19-28
Isaiah 61:1-4, 8-11
Psalm 126 The Lord has done great things for us. (Ps. 126:3)
1 Thessalonians 5:16-24

Having read these readings, consider this:

Mourning and waiting for comfort are the human condition. Right now all the world waits for healing. Christians in the northern hemisphere have taken Advent darkness as a strong and evocative symbol for all human waiting, in all times. The darkness of this season has a certain quiet beauty, especially as it frames the growing presence of holiday lights, but—like John the Baptist—this season is not the light. John then bears witness to the light that is Christ: "Among you stands one whom you do not know." Every Sunday celebrates the presence of the crucified and risen Christ in the power of the Spirit. This third Advent Sunday celebrates how Christ stands present with us all now, hidden in the midst of and sharing all human waiting. Just so, he is already the garland God puts upon the earth, the springing up of righteousness like a blossoming garden, the ground of our rejoicing. In our baptism, in the word we hear today, and in the holy supper, we are clothed like guests at God's marriage with the earth, and we are invited to turn to our mourning and waiting neighbors, being with them in comfort as Jesus Christ is, and working to repair the ruined cities.

FOURTH SUNDAY OF ADVENT

Luke 1:26-38
2 Samuel 7:1-11, 16
Luke 1:46b-55 You, LORD, have lifted up the lowly. (Luke 1:52)
Romans 16:25-27

Having read these readings, consider this:

"The LORD is with you," says Nathan to David. "The Lord is with you," says the angel to Mary. When we hear these readings today, they say to us, "The Lord is with you." We have been and are afraid, especially now. Though we have heard promises about how kings and other rulers will do wonderful things, they have cruelly disappointed our hopes. "Do not be afraid," these readings say to us. The house that God builds is neither a royal temple nor a dynasty of kings, for the true king is not a king at all, but a child born among the poor who grows to become a crucified man and lives as Christ arisen. In the power of the Spirit, he is present now, making any place where his word is heard to be the house of God. That secret is now disclosed. We most usually come to the house God builds when we gather with the assembly to hear the word and to receive Christ in the holy communion. We become God's house, empowered to share Christ with our world. "The Lord is with you." Now. Listen to that word. With Mary, trust it. Say, "Let it be to me according to your word."

NATIVITY OF OUR LORD
CHRISTMAS EVE AND CHRISTMAS DAY

See above, in chapter 1.

FIRST SUNDAY OF CHRISTMAS

Luke 2:22-40
Isaiah 61:10—62:3
Psalm 148 The splendor of the LORD is over earth and heaven. (Ps. 148:13)
Galatians 4:4-7

Having read these readings, consider this:

The texts for the First Sunday of Christmas are painfully honest about death. Two birds—the offering of poor people who could not afford a lamb—are to be ritually killed for the sake of the purification of the mother from the blood of childbirth, but also to stand in for her firstborn son, to redeem him from death. Two old people also show themselves ready to die. And Simeon foretells the death of Jesus, who is in fact not finally redeemed at all, but who himself will be the Lamb who saves us in his cross-death. In all of this, we may hear echoes of our own death: those inner thoughts of ours may be revealed. But listen more deeply: death itself is overcome. The Christ child has come to clothe us in God's salvation, to redeem us. Jesus Christ, born among us, is light for all people, the dawn after night's end. With Anna, we hear the promises of the scripture and sing of the child who saves us. With Simeon, we take the child into our own hands—in the holy communion when that is possible, in the holy scriptures always. That child is now alive among us: Jesus Christ, crucified and risen. God has sent the Spirit of Christ into our hearts so that as free and adopted children of God, together with Christ we may witness to God's mercy in our cities.

SECOND SUNDAY OF CHRISTMAS

See above, in chapter 1.

EPIPHANY OF OUR LORD

See above, in chapter 1.

BAPTISM OF OUR LORD, FIRST SUNDAY AFTER EPIPHANY
SUNDAY, JANUARY 7–13
LECTIONARY 1

Mark 1:4-11
Genesis 1:1-5
Psalm 29 The voice of the LORD is upon the waters. (Ps. 29:3)
Acts 19:1-7

Having read these readings, consider this:

Many people go out to John, confessing their sins and hoping his baptism will be the sign of a new age, an indication of God creating all things anew. We, too, hope for such a new beginning, and we, too, have been baptized, confessing our sins. Jesus also is baptized, hidden among us sinners, joining us in longing for a new age. But in the text, only he sees something utterly new: the torn-open heavens and the descending dove; only he hears the voice of God declaring him the beloved Son. But we hear too! This voice upon the waters comes here, where we are reading these texts. Jesus Christ, whose identity continues to be hidden in Mark's gospel until he is finally hidden by the crucifixion, is revealed to us now as living in the word and sacraments of the church. In encountering Jesus Christ, we see and hear the holy Trinity—the voice from above the heavens, the Son in the water, and the descending Spirit—making all things new, as if the creation of Genesis 1 is all around us again, as if Noah's flood is finally over. Our baptism gathers us into the life of the Trinity, making us, like the ancient Christian Ephesians, witnesses to this new creation.

SECOND SUNDAY AFTER EPIPHANY
SUNDAY, JANUARY 14–20
LECTIONARY 2

John 1:43-51
1 Samuel 3:1-10
Psalm 139:1-6, 13-18 You have searched me out and known me. (Ps. 139:1)
1 Corinthians 6:12-20

Having read these readings, consider this:

Sometimes we feel as if we have no word from God, no vision, no place to come and see what God is doing, no center in a time of alienation. But as the psalm says, God has seen us and known us. More: in our baptism, God has called us, as Samuel, Philip, and Nathanael were called. Listen to these texts more deeply. In Jesus Christ heaven has opened. For us, the angels of God ascend and descend upon him more surely than they did upon Jacob's ancient Bethel (Gen. 28:12). In his death and resurrection, Jesus has become for us the lamp of God, the ark of God, and the house of God where we may come and see. The crucified and risen Christ, present in his word and sacraments in our assembly—and present to us in the scriptures read in our homes—is today the place where we may meet God. Then, gathered into Christ's body by the Holy Spirit, we become together the temple of God, our own bodies now dedicated to bearing witness to God's love for our needy neighbors and for all the world.

THIRD SUNDAY AFTER EPIPHANY
SUNDAY, JANUARY 21–27
LECTIONARY 3

Mark 1:14-20
Jonah 3:1-5, 10
Psalm 62:5-12 God alone is my rock and my salvation. (Ps. 62:6)
1 Corinthians 7:29-31

Having read these readings, consider this:

Our world is full of death and the very real possibility of destruction. Nineveh can be an image for us. Yet after Jonah finally acts on the call of God and speaks God's word to Nineveh, the people immediately repent. That word changes everything! Trusting God, they can live hopefully in their world. After John is arrested, Jesus preaches the nearness of the dominion of God, and the world becomes utterly different for those fishermen. Mark says they "immediately" follow. After Jesus is arrested and killed, the risen Christ once again begins his ministry, coming into our assemblies, speaking the gospel. The dominion of God is near to us because, in the Spirit and through the word, Christ is near to us. We too are called, and the world becomes utterly different for us. We are like fish pulled out of the chaotic sea into the light and air—only, unlike fish, we are made alive together with Christ. We may live "as though not" engaged in the values of the world around us but according to the values of the mercy of God, turning to the needs of our neighbors, inviting them also to live in hope.

FOURTH SUNDAY AFTER EPIPHANY *(if before Transfiguration)* SUNDAY, JANUARY 28–FEBRUARY 3 LECTIONARY 4

Mark 1:21-28
Deuteronomy 18:15-20
Psalm 111 The fear of the LORD is the beginning of wisdom. (Ps. 111:10)
1 Corinthians 8:1-13

Having read these readings, consider this:

There are indeed, right now, false prophets, people who mislead and betray others by what they say, pretending to speak in God's name. We too, as Paul says, can use our religious knowledge to hurt others. How can the fire and the voice of the living God save us from this misuse of religion? Listen. Jesus' teaching ministry begins in an importantly strange way in Mark's gospel. Nothing is said of what he actually teaches. And he oddly silences the unclean spirit who knows who he is. Religious knowledge is already being reworked. In Mark that silence continues through the whole gospel until, at last, Jesus is finally silenced on the cross. But this crucified Jesus is risen, and by the power of the Spirit he comes to our assemblies. He is himself the new teaching, the promised prophet, the fire and voice of God in a way we can encounter. In him God knows us. And the word of this Holy One of God does heal us and turn us in kindness and care toward the others around us.

FIFTH SUNDAY AFTER EPIPHANY *(if before Transfiguration)* SUNDAY, FEBRUARY 4–10 LECTIONARY 5

Mark 1:29-39
Isaiah 40:21-31
Psalm 147:1-11, 20c The LORD heals the brokenhearted. (Ps. 147:3)
1 Corinthians 9:16-23

Having read these readings, consider this:

Mark wants to say in every way he can that God's salvation is hidden in the cross. This is what scholars have called "the messianic secret." There are two instances of the secret in today's text: Jesus silences the demons because they know who he is; and, after "the whole city" has been gathered at his door, he goes away alone to a deserted place. But this hidden Jesus then goes on to all the neighboring towns. In our day, the salvation that is in the cross is still hidden. But we proclaim that the Crucified One is risen and goes on to all the world. He comes here to the house of our church and to our own homes. We are the weak ones, sick with a fever. In the power of the Spirit, Jesus is the presence of the God who strengthens the weak. Jesus is himself the gospel given away for free. We are healed now, so that we—like Peter's mother-in-law—may rise to serve others.

SIXTH SUNDAY AFTER EPIPHANY *(if before Transfiguration)*
SUNDAY, FEBRUARY 11–17
LECTIONARY 6, PROPER 1

Mark 1:40-45
2 Kings 5:1-14
Psalm 30 My God, I cried out to you, and you restored me to health. (Ps. 30:2)
1 Corinthians 9:24-27

Having read these readings, consider this:

All of us long for wholeness of life, ability to run Paul's metaphorical race. One way to achieve that strength, a way we sometimes choose, is the way of power: the king of Aram wants to command and buy health; Naaman longs for powerful and showy miracle-working. It does not work. In the mercy of God, Naaman is instead given the seemingly weak way of the word: he has the counsel of an enslaved girl, and he receives the word sent from a hidden prophet to be combined with the water of the river. Jesus, hidden in the messianic secret and hidden even more in the cross, has joined the weakness of the enslaved girl and of the hidden prophet. Yet he is risen, and his word to us is "I do choose. Be made clean." We too are given the way of the word. In the power of the Spirit, baptism is our Jordan, Jesus our temple and priest, the endless mercy of God our wholeness. Then that word breaks out of hiddenness: it dwells in our homes; it is sung in our assemblies; it is spoken freely in our world so that people may come to it from every quarter.

SEVENTH SUNDAY AFTER EPIPHANY *(if before Transfiguration)* SUNDAY, FEBRUARY 18–24 LECTIONARY 7, PROPER 2

Mark 2:1-12
Isaiah 43:18-25
Psalm 41 Heal me, for I have sinned against you. (Ps. 41:4)
2 Corinthians 1:18-22

Having read these readings, consider this:

We are often paralyzed in our sins. But God is doing yet another new thing. The biblical new things of God are always the old things radically reworked: the exodus through the sea, made water in the wilderness so that the people may return; the sin of the people, made the place where God—I AM—forgives; the death of Jesus on the cross, made his resurrection presence among us now; *no*, made the *yes* to all of God's promises. The house where our friends may bring us or where we may bring others in need can be found wherever this word is read, but it is found especially in the Sunday assembly. There the Risen One continues his healing ministry especially by enacting the forgiveness of sins, the very forgiveness that can indeed be given only by God. There we hear and eat and drink the *yes* of God and respond with the "amen." There the Spirit is given into our hearts as seal and pledge of all that God is doing. We are drawn into the life of the holy Trinity. We may need to keep on remodeling the house so that others may come.

EIGHTH SUNDAY AFTER EPIPHANY *(if before Transfiguration)* SUNDAY, FEBRUARY 25–MARCH 1 LECTIONARY 8, PROPER 3

Mark 2:13-22
Hosea 2:14-20
Psalm 103:1-13, 22 LORD, you are full of compassion and mercy. (Ps. 103:8)
2 Corinthians 3:1-6

Having read these readings, consider this:

One of the most important images from the Old Testament proposes that God will marry Israel. God is no *Baal*, the Canaanite divine name that images the divine to be a harsh master; God is rather to be seen as a faithful and loving spouse. The earth itself will celebrate this covenant of marriage: vineyards will thrive; humanity will have peace with wild beasts; war will be no more. This image stands behind the metaphors in the passage from Mark read today: Jesus is bridegroom, physician, new wine. Only now, surprisingly, the participants in the wedding banquet and the ones being healed are sinners and tax collectors. As the story goes on, we see this bridegroom killed. But we believe he is risen and present to us in the word that we read and in the assembly. There his meal is the wedding banquet open to us sinners. There his Spirit writes God's faithfulness, love, and mercy on our hearts. There we are made messengers of the new covenant: God intends to be married to all the earth, bringing about the very justice and peace imaged in Hosea. Our actions with each other and with the earth itself can celebrate this wedding.

TRANSFIGURATION OF OUR LORD
LAST SUNDAY AFTER EPIPHANY

Mark 9:2-9
2 Kings 2:1-12
Psalm 50:1-6 Out of Zion, perfect in beauty, God shines forth in glory. (Ps. 50:2)
2 Corinthians 4:3-6

Having read these readings, consider this:

In the Gospel according to Mark, the identity of Jesus—who Jesus really is—is repeatedly hidden in a secret. Here, in today's text, after Peter and the others see Jesus in shining clothing talking with Moses and Elijah—the two Old Testament figures who were taken to be with God, the two who stand for all the law and the prophets—and after they hear the very voice of God bearing witness to him, they then see only Jesus—just the man Jesus—and he tells them to say nothing until after the resurrection. Though they do not understand, they will soon enough see him killed, hidden in death. Now, this Sunday as every Sunday, we gather on the day of resurrection. And the hidden truth is to be told openly in our assemblies and in our homes. Mark's gospel is that truth being told now. In its text, also we hear the voice from the mountain. In the power of the Spirit, the light of Jesus Christ shines in our hearts. What we see is not only the shining Son of God, but the Jesus who has gone to the cross, God with us in our suffering. That is the secret. Acting out of that hidden light, we are invited to join Paul in serving others.

ASH WEDNESDAY

See above, in chapter 2.

FIRST SUNDAY IN LENT

Mark 1:9-15
Genesis 9:8-17
Psalm 25:1-10 Your paths, O LORD, are steadfast love and faithfulness. (Ps. 25:10)
1 Peter 3:18-22

Having read these readings, consider this:

Here are metaphors for how we are right now: We are in a flood, drowning. We are wandering in the wilderness, afraid of the wild beasts, and if we are being tested, we fail. We are surrounded by death, and that imprisons us. But Jesus Christ comes preaching, and in the power of the Spirit he comes to us now. His coming changes everything. Jesus has seen the dove descending, the end of the flood. Baptized into him, we also receive the Spirit. Jesus' resistance to the evil one turns our wildernesses into places of peace with all creation, places where the angels serve. Baptized into him, we see our world with new eyes and are given strength to resist evil and take joy in the creation. Jesus' cross and resurrection break open the captivity of death. Baptized into his death, we are raised with him out of fear. The forty days of Lent invite us to remember again that we are baptized, to rejoice in God's rainbow covenant with all creatures, and to be ourselves part of the sign of God's love for the world.

SECOND SUNDAY IN LENT

Mark 8:31-38
Genesis 17:1-7, 15-16
Psalm 22:23-31 All the ends of the earth shall remember and turn to the LORD. (Ps. 22:27)
Romans 4:13-25

Having read these readings, consider this:

In Mark, Jesus' identity is a secret until it is told openly in the church after his death and resurrection. But in today's gospel reading, the first of three "passion predictions" in Mark, Jesus speaks boldly and openly about that coming death. All three of the passion predictions are accompanied with words about our discipleship. Today, resisting Peter, Jesus makes clear that this discipleship involves honesty about death. "Taking up the cross" is not self-torture. There is already enough suffering in the world. Rather, it is telling the truth that we die, and it is being ready to suffer for the gospel if we must. So Peter did suffer martyrdom. But death is never the last word. By the power of the Spirit poured out from Christ's death, we are brought to faith like the faith of Abraham—trust in the God who gives life to the dead; trust from two old people who were "as good as dead." In the resurrection, Jesus our Lord is made alive. By baptism God makes us alive together with Christ. Like Abraham and Sarah, we too are given a new identity: we are named children of God and co-heirs with Christ. And we are turned in love and service toward the many people who are being invited also to trust in God like Abraham and Sarah.

THIRD SUNDAY IN LENT

John 2:13-22
Exodus 20:1-17
Psalm 19 The commandment of the LORD gives light to the eyes. (Ps. 19:8)
1 Corinthians 1:18-25

Having read these readings, consider this:

While we may not buy cattle or doves to give to God, we too sometimes turn our religion into a negotiation with the divine—"I give to you, O God, so that you must give to me"—and we too sometimes seek to profit, like the moneychangers, from other people's religious negotiations. Christ ends all that. Though it looks like foolishness, his cross is the wisdom and power of God and the end of negotiations. Risen, he is our temple, the very place we meet God in the power of the Spirit. What happens in that place, that temple which is assembly in Christ, is that God gives to us so that we may turn and give to others. When we were baptized into that house of God, the ten commandments were given to us as part of being baptized. They are a lively agenda for us, especially if, with Martin Luther, we continually reinterpret them for the present time. This agenda is founded in God's thousandfold mercy, in which such mercy becomes our own way. Rather than coveting someone else's things, we engage in almsgiving. Rather than lying about someone else, we pray for them. Rather than misusing someone else, we fast from self-indulgence. And in it all Jesus Christ is our sabbath rest. The way of these commandments is the way of Lent and a way of joy. Such religion is light to our eyes.

FOURTH SUNDAY IN LENT

John 3:14-21
Numbers 21:4-9
Psalm 107:1-3, 17-22 You deliver your people from their distress. (Ps. 107:19)
Ephesians 2:1-10

Having read these readings, consider this:

The writers of the New Testament sought in many ways to present the meaning of the crucifixion of Jesus, a tragic event that at first seems too horrible to have any meaning. The Gospel according to John here means to transform our horror into hope, borrowing an image from the Old Testament to do so. In Numbers, the people are dying, and serpents are causing this death. At God's command, the serpent on the pole, as if it were death enthroned, gives life. The people look and live. So for us, the man executed on the cross gives life to the world. We all are dead in sin. Christ shares the worst of our deaths. Now, not by looking but by looking in faith, by trusting what God has done, we are made alive together with Christ. The Spirit, poured out in baptism, lifts us up together with Christ into life. God loves the world and, giving us that gift of love, enables us also to love others with our good works.

FIFTH SUNDAY IN LENT

John 12:20-33
Jeremiah 31:31-34
Psalm 51:1-12 Create in me a clean heart, O God. (Ps. 51:10)
Hebrews 5:5-10

Having read these readings, consider this:

Things fall apart. People break their covenant with God. We sin. We die. But "come and see," says the Gospel according to John. And along with the Greeks and Philip and Andrew, here at the end of Lent in the Christian assembly, we do. We see the cross. We see that Jesus' being lifted up is at the same time his death and his glorification. He is the falling seed that becomes a huge harvest. What we think is an awful death has become the center that draws all things and all people into a new unity in God as if God has married them in a new covenant. The sufferings of Christ have become the source of eternal salvation. In baptism we have been drawn into that salvation, marked with that cross, made part of that new covenant, made alive. In baptism we have received the very Spirit poured out from Christ, and we have been forgiven. Exactly in God's forgiveness, all of us—least and greatest, wise and not so wise—come to know who God really is. Then we ourselves can learn to turn with forgiveness to our neighbors.

SUNDAY OF THE PASSION, PALM SUNDAY

See above, in chapter 2.

THE THREE DAYS
MAUNDY THURSDAY, GOOD FRIDAY, VIGIL OF EASTER

See above, in chapter 2.

RESURRECTION OF OUR LORD, EASTER DAY

Mark 16:1-8
Isaiah 25:6-9
Psalm 118:1-2, 14-24 This is the day that the Lord has made; let us rejoice and be glad in it. (Ps. 118:24)
1 Corinthians 15:1-11

Having read these readings, consider this:

All around us and in us are death and tears. One medieval image of death was as a huge mouth swallowing people up by the hundreds, and that image seems apt today. But the promise of Isaiah is that God will instead swallow up death itself, wipe away tears from all faces, and spread a feast for all the nations. The resurrection of Jesus Christ is the beginning of that feast. But the Gospel according to Mark ends with only an announcement ("he has been raised") and a promise ("there you will see him"), seemingly without an appearance of the risen Christ. Then we read Mark again and note that Jesus comes into Galilee, preaches in Galilee, heals and forgives in Galilee, holds meetings in Galilee. Reading the book, we see him in Galilee. The gospel book is itself his appearance. We in the assembly have the same announcement and promise: as we read the story of Jesus, he is with us, with us in all the scriptures, adding us to the list of witnesses. We are welcomed to the feast of the end of death. Empowered by God's Spirit, we can join in wiping away tears from our neighbors' faces.

SECOND SUNDAY OF EASTER

John 20:19-31
Acts 4:32-35
Psalm 133 How good and pleasant it is to live together in unity. (Ps. 133:1)
1 John 1:1—2:2

Having read these readings, consider this:

We see and sometimes touch wounds all around us, but these wounds are not usually life-giving. They are our own wounds and wounds we have caused in others. They are the wounds of a suffering humanity. They are also the wounds the earth has suffered, not least at our hands. They are signs of our sin. But Sunday after Sunday, through word and sacrament, we encounter Jesus Christ, and we discover that he shares our wounds. He is risen, but the wounds of his crucifixion have not disappeared. These signs of God sharing our need and death have become instead the source of the Holy Spirit giving life, of forgiveness proclaimed to us and by us to others, and of peace in shared community. In faith, we may see and touch those life-giving wounds by hearing the scriptures, by celebrating the holy communion, and by turning in empathy and with shared resources to our neighbors and our world.

THIRD SUNDAY OF EASTER

Luke 24:36b-48
Acts 3:12-19
Psalm 4 The LORD does wonders for the faithful. (Ps. 4:3)
1 John 3:1-7

Having read these readings, consider this:

The author of Acts, in seeking to appeal to the Gentiles and exonerate Pilate, has Peter blaming "the Israelites" for the death of Jesus. Peter here does not even remember his own guilt. The Christian tradition has rather seen the death of Jesus, however it came about, as bringing the possibility of repentance and forgiveness to us all. The scriptures are closed to us when we use them to judge others for their sins, forgetting our own. But the risen Christ in the power of the Spirit opens our minds to understand the scriptures. In them, when they are truly opened, we see his wounds and encounter his resurrection. In them we see the risen Jesus eat a fish, that representation of the chaos of the sea—of death—made into life-giving food. Every Sunday, the scriptures are opened for us. And every Sunday, when we are able to gather, Christ gives us life in his meal, his death made into our life. When we cannot gather, we eat his body and blood in the scriptures themselves, by faith. In word and sacrament, we meet the Author of life and are given forgiveness, made children of God, and sent with words of witness and forgiveness to others.

FOURTH SUNDAY OF EASTER

John 10:11-18
Acts 4:5-12
Psalm 23 The LORD is my shepherd; I shall not be in want. (Ps. 23:1)
1 John 3:16-24

Having read these readings, consider this:

In the ancient Near East, kings and other leaders were often compared with shepherds. But many of them were quite awful, serving only themselves, misleading and betraying and even forsaking the people. They would often destroy instead of working to build. We too sometimes have bad leaders. We may even be tempted to support them. Or we may ourselves be such leaders. But Jesus Christ, crucified and risen, is the good shepherd. He does his "shepherding"—his knowing and leading us—by laying down his life in love, by staying with us, sharing our need and our death, and never running away. By the Spirit which God gives us through the scriptures—as also through the water of baptism and the overflowing cup of the eucharist—we know Jesus and his healing name. Even in times of separation, the risen Christ draws us together into unity as one flock with the one true shepherd. Saved from ourselves and from bad leadership, we are formed to believe in the name of Jesus, to love each other, and to give ourselves to our neighbor's needs.

FIFTH SUNDAY OF EASTER

John 15:1-8
Acts 8:26-40
Psalm 22:25-31 All the ends of the earth shall remember and turn to the LORD. (Ps. 22:27)
1 John 4:7-21

Having read these readings, consider this:

Jesus Christ is the true vine, but we are too often withered branches, afraid and without the fruit of love. This day let the word of God do its cleansing, pruning work. In that word, you—whether alone or gathered with an assembly of disciples—are connected to the crucified and risen Christ, and God's own Spirit flows to you. You are made alive and part of Christ for the life of the world. This day let Philip explain the scriptures also to you. Remember that, with the Ethiopian eunuch, you are baptized. Remember that you have drunk from Christ the vine at the eucharist. Abide in Christ and let his word abide in you. Then, even now when the world is filled with fear, put fear away and turn in love toward your neighbors, especially toward those whom others may consider outsiders, learning from and with them, helping to enable justice for them.

SIXTH SUNDAY OF EASTER

John 15:9-17
Acts 10:44-48
Psalm 98 Shout with joy to the LORD, all you lands. (Ps. 98:4)
1 John 5:1-6

Having read these readings, consider this:

As in the synoptic gospels, both the Gospel according to John and the First Letter of John articulate two commandments: we should love God, and we should love each other. But even if these commandments are "not burdensome," we often do not keep them. Are we then really children and friends of God? In answer to our failure and sin, God gives the witness that overcomes the world: the Spirit, the water, and the blood. The Spirit enables us to trust that Jesus comes among us by the water of his baptism and by the blood of his cross. More: these things come to us, when we are in assembly and even when we are alone. As Jesus dies, he gives over the Spirit to be among us and teach us. The water has not been withheld from us, and like Cornelius and his family, we have been baptized into him. We have received and we will receive again his blood in the holy communion. Spirit, water, and blood testify to us that we are indeed children of God, forgiven and formed anew as friends to turn to our neighbor in love.

ASCENSION OF OUR LORD, THE FORTIETH DAY OF EASTER

See above, in chapter 2.

SEVENTH SUNDAY OF EASTER

John 17:6-19
Acts 1:15-17, 21-26
Psalm 1 The LORD knows the way of the righteous. (Ps. 1:6)
1 John 5:9-13

Having read these readings, consider this:

Every year, on the Seventh Sunday of Easter, we read a passage from the long prayer of Jesus that John's gospel situates on the eve of the crucifixion. With its simple religious language, the prayer proclaims the meaning of Jesus' death and resurrection. But we easily misunderstand: while we should indeed seek to keep God's word and to unite with all Christians, this text is not about that. Nor is it about us trying to avoid the world. Rather, in this text the word of God keeps us. The name of God already holds us in unity. And among the words that Jesus has given us is this: God loves the world. In John's gospel, the "world" is a name for all things organized as if there were no God. But Jesus Christ has been sent into that world, and his cross has marked all things with God's saving love. Now, in the power of the Spirit and with the apostle Matthias, we too are sent as witnesses to that love. With the First Letter of John we know that this love of God gives us eternal life already, now. Eternal life does not wait until after death but is the joyful communal sharing of Christ's truth now.

DAY OF PENTECOST, THE FIFTIETH DAY OF EASTER

John 15:26-27; 16:4b-15
Ezekiel 37:1-14
Psalm 104:24-34, 35b Send forth your Spirit and renew the face of the earth. (Ps. 104:30)
Acts 2:1-21

Having read these readings, consider this:

Amid the memory of widespread ill health, and amid continuing national and international troubles, we may feel like the people in exile: bones dried up, hope lost, cut off completely. The death of Jesus may seem like another sad story, far away from helping us. But on this fiftieth day of the Easter feast—Pentecost—the Spirit of God who bears witness to God's victory in the cross is poured into our hearts. With that Spirit comes the whole Easter gospel: Christ is alive, we are raised up with him to no longer be afraid, and the Spirit empowers us to join the witness to Jesus' resurrection. This Spirit puts life and hope and new breath within us—in the word we read today, in the remembrance of our baptism into Christ, and in the holy supper when we receive it in the assembly. In faith, we see the face of the weary earth being renewed, and we join the renewal by turning in love to our neighbors.

THE HOLY TRINITY
FIRST SUNDAY AFTER PENTECOST

John 3:1-17
Isaiah 6:1-8
Psalm 29 Worship the Lord in the beauty of holinesss. (Ps. 29:2)
Romans 8:12-17

Having read these readings, consider this:

Both in reading these passages of scripture today and in gathering for eucharist, we find ourselves standing before God, the Thrice-Holy One. In both places we should cry out with Isaiah, "Woe is me! I am a person of unclean lips, dwelling among people of unclean lips, and I cannot stand before God and live!" But the holy Trinity gathers us into mercy: the Spirit gives us birth in baptism and forms us to pray; Jesus Christ is sent to share our death and our life, making us joint heirs of hope; the Father, the one who sends

Jesus, loves the world and sends us with him as witnesses. There are not three gods, but one loving, rich, enfolding mystery. The Trinity is the living God we know, whose divine life we are drawn to share. With the word of these scriptures—as also with the bread and cup of the eucharist—the coal has touched our lips, and we can turn with good news and love toward our neighbors.

SUNDAY, MAY 24–28 *(if after Holy Trinity)*
LECTIONARY 8, PROPER 3

See above, at Eighth Sunday after Epiphany, February 25–March 1.

SUNDAY, MAY 29–JUNE 4 *(if after Holy Trinity)*
LECTIONARY 9, PROPER 4

Mark 2:23—3:6
Deuteronomy 5:12-15
Psalm 81:1-10 Raise a loud shout to the God of Jacob. (Ps. 81:1)
2 Corinthians 4:5-12

Having read these readings, consider this:

According to Deuteronomy, God acted to liberate enslaved people with "a mighty hand." According to Mark, humanity sometimes has a withered hand, a symbol for a broken and partial life. We should see that we have the withered hand, in need of the outstretched arm of God. With Paul, the "clay jars" of our bodies are full of death. Then note: in Deuteronomy, unlike Exodus, the purpose of the sabbath is a rest for all, including the poor, commemorating God's action to give those who were enslaved wholeness in life. In Mark, Jesus takes authority to make the sabbath a day of such wholeness: food for the hungry, healing for the broken. The gospel today reflects ancient Christian attitudes toward religious law: what is sacred must always include care for those in need. The reading then begins to point toward Jesus' death. When we gather on Sunday, that crucified and risen Lord Jesus Christ is himself our sabbath, our bread of the presence, our hope for healing. By the power of the Spirit, the light of God's glory in the face of Christ shines with life into our hearts. Our sacred assembly must then turn toward a world in need of God's rest.

SUNDAY, JUNE 5–11 *(if after Holy Trinity)* LECTIONARY 10, PROPER 5

Mark 3:20-35
Genesis 3:8-15
Psalm 130 Wait for the LORD, for with the LORD there is steadfast love. (Ps. 130:7)
2 Corinthians 4:13—5:1

Having read these readings, consider this:

We all are the woman and the man in the old legend about the beginning of sin: we are afraid; we blame each other; we blame the serpent; we blame even God. Evil is very strong, and we find ourselves trapped in its house. But Jesus Christ, in the power of the Spirit, can pull us out of that house. Though he is mocked by others—even his own family—and though he is finally killed, by his cross he plunders the house of evil. The grace of God in his death and resurrection makes of us a new and eternal house, a place of thanksgiving. When we hear the scriptures today, we are with Jesus in his house. He calls us his new family. We see that house when we are able to gather with others around word and sacrament. Formed by his word and by that gathering with him, we turn to do the will of God in loving our neighbors.

SUNDAY, JUNE 12–18 *(if after Holy Trinity)* LECTIONARY 11, PROPER 6

Mark 4:26-34
Ezekiel 17:22-24
Psalm 92:1-4, 12-15 The righteous shall spread abroad like a cedar of Lebanon. (Ps. 92:12)
2 Corinthians 5:6-10, 14-17

Having read these readings, consider this:

According to Mark, the explanation of the parables was given secretly to the disciples. But now this meaning is proclaimed openly in the church: God makes what is low and dry to be high and green. The central occasion of this action of God is found in the cross. Walking by sight and not by faith, we all too often live only for ourselves, and we give special attention to people who appear high and powerful, as if they were the source of more life for us. But just as an annual bush—a scraggly bush that dies—is presented by Jesus as the very tree of life, just as the dry seed becomes a mighty harvest, just as God makes a sprig to be a mighty cedar, so against all appearances the cross of Christ's death holds us into a new creation. In the word proclaimed in the assembly today, the Holy Spirit brings us to nest by faith in the tree of life which is Jesus Christ crucified and risen. We eat and drink the fruit of that tree. Then we are invited to live not for ourselves but for him and for all the needy world which he loves.

SUNDAY, JUNE 19–25 *(if after Holy Trinity)* LECTIONARY 12, PROPER 7

Mark 4:35-41
Job 38:1-11
Psalm 107:1-3, 23-32 You stilled the storm and silenced the waves of the sea. (Ps. 107:29)
2 Corinthians 6:1-13

Having read these readings, consider this:

Let the storm at sea stand for all that threatens life, for evil, and for death. Today's readings are full of such threats. Paul's life has been marked by afflictions, some of which sound familiar to us: hardships, calamities, riots, sleepless nights. The whole book of Job tells the story of a man of suffering whose very life cries out to God. And the disciples in the boat are afraid, complaining to Jesus. We are in the same boat, and we too are often afraid. At first Jesus seems to be quite hidden, asleep, silent. But then, with the disciples, we discover that all the power of God to create and hold all things—the very power that answered Job by appearing in the whirlwind—is found in Jesus Christ. Just so, in Mark, Jesus seems to be hidden in suffering on the cross. But now is the day of salvation. By the power of the Spirit, the Risen One is with us in our gathering, in our reading of the scriptures, and in our keeping of his meal. In that presence, God says to all that threatens life, "Thus far and no farther!" Opening our hearts wide to that word, we also open our hearts wide to our neighbors' need. With Paul, we are dying, and see—we are alive!

SUNDAY, JUNE 26–JULY 2
LECTIONARY 13, PROPER 8

Mark 5:21-43
Lamentations 3:22-33
Psalm 30 I will exalt you, O Lord, because you have lifted me up. (Ps. 30:1)
2 Corinthians 8:7-15

Having read these readings, consider this:

The Gospel according to Mark continues to be the book of secret epiphanies. We see God's life-giving presence revealed, but in what seem to be secret places. Hidden in a fleeting touch amid a crushing crowd, locked away in a room with only a few other people, and concealed by Jesus' own command to tell no one, is God's power to heal and to raise the dead—the very steadfast love of the Lord that never ceases. Just so, the hope for life was hidden in the cross. Also at the cross, Jesus was mocked. Also in his death by crucifixion, Jesus was made unclean. But this Hidden One is now raised from the dead himself: present to our assemblies and present in our open reading of these stories. We all are the hemorrhaging woman. We all are the dead girl and the grieving parents. He calls our assemblies to attend to the suffering of women and to respect any whom society marginalizes, just as he did. By the power of the Spirit in the eucharist we all together are given something to eat, food for life. Out of the poverty of Jesus comes our enrichment with a wealth that may now flow from us to others who have been waiting in silence with their bleeding needs.

SUNDAY, JULY 3–9
LECTIONARY 14, PROPER 9

Mark 6:1-13
Ezekiel 2:1-5
Psalm 123 Our eyes look to you, O God, until you show us your mercy. (Ps. 123:2)
2 Corinthians 12:2-10

Having read these readings, consider this:

We are the rebellious house, the ones who refuse to hear. But among us is the prophet who heals us and our sick ones nonetheless. As Mark tells the story, Jesus is reduced to utter weakness, able to do no miraculous deed of power at all when he is in his hometown, among those who presume that they know him. Except, out of that weakness he does still heal the sick, even amid all the unbelief. Then his weakness becomes the source of the sending of the Twelve, and they, though they have nothing, preach and heal with power. These Markan stories are images of the cross and resurrection of Jesus: hidden in the weakness of Jesus, supposedly known and yet rejected in his death, is the very power of Christ, dwelling now among us in word and sacrament. Following Christ, Paul says that whenever he was weak, then he was strong. As we listen to this word of God, the Spirit also enters into us and we rise. Out of our own weakness, having nothing except the gospel, we may turn to our neighbors in witness and in service.

SUNDAY, JULY 10–16
LECTIONARY 15, PROPER 10

Mark 6:14-29
Amos 7:7-15
Psalm 85:8-13 I will listen to what the Lord God is saying. (Ps. 85:8)
Ephesians 1:3-14

Having read these readings, consider this:

The gospel tells of an ugly birthday banquet that fully displays Herod's tortured psychology: he is fascinated by John; he shows off before his guests; he lusts after his stepdaughter; yet throughout, he is deeply afraid. The result is murder. And when he hears about Jesus, it is his continuing guilt that responds. The story may be for us like Amos's plumbline set against the crookedness of all unjust and despotic regimes. It may also measure out the ways we ourselves have acted from cowardice, self-importance, and guilt. But in the gospel, the story is also the negative image of another banquet, the one in Mark 14:3-9: there an unnamed woman does not demand Jesus' head on a platter but faithfully anoints his head, thus preparing his "body beforehand for its burial." That act leads us to another meal, the meal which proclaims Jesus' cross and resurrection, the meal where he today gives himself to us. In that meal, as in the whole word of the gospel, the grace and love of God, "freely bestowed on us in the Beloved," are on full display. Listening to God speaking peace in Jesus, and marked by the seal of the Spirit in word and sacrament, we turn in that love and peace toward our needy and harassed world.

SUNDAY, JULY 17–23
LECTIONARY 16, PROPER 11

Mark 6:30-34, 53-56
Jeremiah 23:1-6
Psalm 23 The LORD is my shepherd; I shall not be in want. (Ps. 23:1)
Ephesians 2:11-22

Having read these readings, consider this:

We are all like sheep without a shepherd. Indeed, our whole world society has leaders and rulers—for whom Jeremiah uses the classic Old Testament metaphor of "shepherds"—that scatter, divide, and alienate us from each other, creating hostility. We are easily tempted to live without hope and as if there were no God in the world. But God promises to gather and lead the flock until it comes to fruitfulness and fearlessness. Fulfilling that promise, Jesus comes into our midst with compassion. He teaches; he prepares a table before us; he heals the many sick; and he raises up other shepherds among us to give us these very things from him and from his death and resurrection. With these actions God shepherds the scattered flock. If we are alone, simply hearing the word of Christ leads and restores us. In assembly, by the power of the Spirit the word, the bread, and the peace of Jesus Christ again and again gather us into unity. We are made the house of the Lord, the dwelling place of God. And we are sent to help lead others out of division, mutual hostility, and fear.

SUNDAY, JULY 24–30
LECTIONARY 17, PROPER 12

John 6:1-21
2 Kings 4:42-44
Psalm 145:10-18 You open wide your hand and satisfy the desire of every living thing. (Ps. 145:16)
Ephesians 3:14-21

Having read these readings, consider this:

How can we find food enough to feed all the hungry world? And though we ourselves may not often be as physically hungry as countless people are, do we realize we also are part of that world, needing help? In the story, Jesus feeds a multitude; like Elijah, he uses just a little of the humble bread of the poor. But Jesus is more than a miracle-working prophet. He is himself the very bread that we need. The wilderness blossoms; the sea is made a place to walk; the God of the old Passover story—I AM—is with us. Yet when they want to make him a king, he hides, just as his divinity will later be hidden on the cross. In faith, we know that the Bread of God comes to us from that cross—in the meal that witnesses to his death and resurrection, as also in the word that is full of God's presence and love. By the Spirit working in word and sacrament, Christ comes to dwell in our hearts, and we are filled with the fullness of God. Then we are made to be what we hear and eat. As the church, we take up the twelve baskets to distribute the bread of love in the needy world.

SUNDAY, JULY 31–AUGUST 6
LECTIONARY 18, PROPER 13

John 6:24-35
Exodus 16:2-4, 9-15
Psalm 78:23-29 God rained down manna from heaven; so mortals ate the bread of angels. (Ps. 78:24, 25)
Ephesians 4:1-16

Having read these readings, consider this:

These texts invite us to Christian maturity by mercifully correcting our complaining, our blaming others, and our listening to conspiracy theories. "What is it?"—*mah-na*? in Hebrew—the Israelites said of the desert bread on the ground. "How can there be food here?" It was bread from God, bread in a place where there could not be bread since there were no grainfields and no bakeries in the wilderness. In the story, God gave unexpected life to the people who had been liberated. God still gives life where we thought life could not be. The cross of Christ is for us, against all expectation, the source of life. Jesus Christ, crucified and risen, is the life-giving bread, and that bread of life is available to us all in the holy scriptures and in the holy supper in the church. God the Father sets the table; Christ is the food; the Holy Spirit is the server. Made one in that Spirit, we are gifted by Christ with skills to serve others with the Bread of God, with life where people thought there could be none.

SUNDAY, AUGUST 7–13
LECTIONARY 19, PROPER 14

John 6:35, 41-51
I Kings 19:4-8
Psalm 34:1-8 Taste and see that the LORD is good. (Ps. 34:8)
Ephesians 4:25—5:2

Having read these readings, consider this:

This Sunday the Letter to the Ephesians calls us to speak the truth to each other. Part of the truth is that, like Elijah, we all become weary, discouraged, despairing even. We are indeed no better than our ancestors. But the story says that there was bread for Elijah, and in the strength of that food he was able to revive and go to Horeb, the mountain where God had met Moses, the mountain where God was to be seen. Is there bread also for us? Yes. The word of the scriptures today is like the voice of the angel calling us to get up and eat. And the presence of Jesus Christ, crucified and risen, in both word and sacrament is the very bread of life. "Taste and see," the psalm calls out. "Taste and see" was the old Christian invitation to holy communion. Eating this bread enables seeing! If we eat the word of the scriptures in our homes and the word and meal of God in the church, what will we see? We will see the very humanity of Jesus—his flesh—given away and forming us to live in love. We will see the Spirit of God sealing us together as witnesses to grace. Taught of God, we will see that God is good.

SUNDAY, AUGUST 14–20
LECTIONARY 20, PROPER 15

John 6:51-58
Proverbs 9:1-6
Psalm 34:9-14 Those who seek the LORD lack nothing that is good. (Ps. 34:10)
Ephesians 5:15-20

Having read these readings, consider this:

Because the days are evil, the Letter to the Ephesians urges us to be wise, not foolish, not drunk in our fear of death. In Proverbs, Wisdom herself—the very word by which God made the universe with its seven pillars, its seven visible planets—calls us to lay aside our immaturity and live with the insight that accords with the deep structure of all things. But where is that wisdom? Can it really be eaten and drunk as at a banquet? For John's gospel, the Word through which all things came into being has become flesh in Jesus Christ. He has died with us. He lives with us. And he gives his very existence to us—his flesh and blood—in his word and in his meal in the church. Wisdom's banquet is there, in word and sacrament. Then living in maturity and wisdom, in accord with the universe—truly living—looks like this: singing together in the Spirit; giving thanks to the Father always for all things through Jesus Christ; and, in the Spirit of that thanksgiving, turning with compassion and forgiveness toward our neighbor and in diligent care toward the earth itself.

SUNDAY, AUGUST 21–27
LECTIONARY 21, PROPER 16

John 6:56-69
Joshua 24:1-2a, 14-18
Psalm 34:15-22 *The eyes of the Lord are upon the righteous. (Ps. 34:15)*
Ephesians 6:10-20

Having read these readings, consider this:

For the past four Sundays we have heard from the lectionary that Jesus truly gives himself to us and that he does so like multiplied loaves; like bread in the wilderness, where we thought bread could not be, like food that enables us to see God; and like Wisdom's feast, healing our foolishness. On this Sunday we read once more from the Bread of Life chapter of John's gospel. Only, now we are called not to turn away from this gift, however offensive Jesus' language may seem, however difficult it is to believe that his death for us is food and drink, his flesh and blood the way he abides in us, his word life-giving bread. The form of Peter's confession in this fourth gospel is here: Jesus Christ has the words of eternal life. We join with Joshua and with Peter to cleave to this life, not letting it go—or rather, it does not let us go. By the gift of the Spirit we are clothed with it: truth, righteousness, faith, the promise of salvation, and the very word of God all become "armor" for us as we engage in a strange sort of battle: stopping evil, doing whatever enables us to proclaim peace for our world, and persevering in prayer for all of God's people. Christ feeds us. The Spirit outfits us. God holds us and sends us. So each of us and the whole assembly are gathered into the Trinity.

SUNDAY, AUGUST 28–SEPTEMBER 3
LECTIONARY 22, PROPER 17

Mark 7:1-8, 14-15, 21-23
Deuteronomy 4:1-2, 6-9
Psalm 15 Lord, who may dwell in your tabernacle? (Ps. 15:1)
James 1:17-27

Having read these readings, consider this:

Of course we will wash our hands, wash food that comes from the market, wash our cups and plates. But we fool ourselves if we think that such washing makes us pure before God. Jesus is right to teach that evil comes from within ourselves. And religions focused on purity practices frequently intend to exclude others and exalt ourselves, thinking the others to be polluted and ourselves to be clean. That is the real stain on the religious world. But the one who teaches about the origin of evil in Mark 7 is also the one who generously gives away bread to the hungry and gives himself away at the cross. Risen among us, giving bread and forgiveness in our assemblies, he is the one who may dwell in the tabernacle of God. By the power of the Spirit, giving us new birth in the word, Jesus brings us also to dwell with him before God. Religion that flows from that implanted word will be about caring for those who most obviously cannot care for themselves and about avoiding the stain of religious practices that exclude. Such will be the law that we teach our children and our children's children.

SUNDAY, SEPTEMBER 4–10
LECTIONARY 23, PROPER 18

Mark 7:24-37
Isaiah 35:4-7a
Psalm 146 I will praise the Lord as long as I live. (Ps. 146:2)
James 2:1-17

Having read these readings, consider this:

In our world, with widespread violence and sickness, with our own and our children's illnesses, with our inability to hear each other and to speak clearly, it is hard to say truthfully, "Here is your God!" Rather, here is your need of God! God seems as hidden as Jesus sought to be in that house, as hidden as Jesus finally was on the cross. But Christ is risen and present with us in the assembly-house of the church or in our own homes when we read the scriptures with the church. His resurrection is openly proclaimed among us. In faith, we may come with the woman, praying for all in need and insisting that God's no become a yes, God's hiddenness become God's healing presence. Empowered by the Spirit, the word of the gospel and the water of baptism open our ears to hear and our mouths to speak in love. In the holy communion, when we are able to gather, the crumbs from the Lord's table fall to us. Here indeed is your God! We are then called to let the assembly-house of the church show forth the gracious presence of this triune God by offering free welcome to all and by sending not just words but concrete help to people in need.

SUNDAY, SEPTEMBER 11–17
LECTIONARY 24, PROPER 19

Mark 8:27-38
Isaiah 50:4-9a
Psalm 116:1-9 I will walk in the presence of the Lord. (Ps. 116:9)
James 3:1-12

Having read these readings, consider this:

The gospel today is the first of the three "passion predictions" in Mark. It invites us to remember that crucifixion intended not only to kill but also to publicly shame those regarded as the most despicable criminals. Many early Christians were indeed ashamed of Jesus' death, resisting the idea that it happened, as Peter does in the text. They were also afraid that it could happen to them. So, we also often turn away in fear for ourselves from people who are profoundly suffering. But Jesus, like the servant in the song in Isaiah, does not hide from insult and spitting, instead quite openly speaking about it. He is truly the Messiah that Peter confesses, but in a hidden way. Trusting God, Jesus gives himself into suffering with the suffering ones. Only now, because of his presence with us and in the assembly, does the truth of his vindication by God stand forth in clarity: Christ is risen, and in the power of the Spirit, he is himself the blessing-word that sustains the weary. Hearing that word, we ourselves begin again to pay attention to the suffering in the world, seeking to be a blessing to our neighbors rather than a curse. "Taking up the cross" does not mean making more suffering in the world. It does mean not hiding in fear and shame from the suffering that is there. We will walk in the presence of the Lord, who rescues our life from death.

SUNDAY, SEPTEMBER 18–24
LECTIONARY 25, PROPER 20

Mark 9:30-37
Jeremiah 11:18-20
Psalm 54 God is my helper; it is the Lord who sustains my life. (Ps. 54:4)
James 3:13—4:3, 7-8a

Having read these readings, consider this:

On this Sunday, we come to the second "passion prediction," the central one of the three in Mark. It is indeed centrally important. The misunderstanding and arguing of the disciples echo the conflicts and disputes, envy and ambition in the congregation of which James writes. We are ourselves accused by both Mark and James: we too argue with each other; we too put ourselves first; we too are unwilling to yield. But Jesus Christ is himself the one who is last of all and servant of all, the lamb led to the slaughter. As he is hidden in his secret teaching about the cross, so he is hidden in death itself, as if his name would be no longer remembered. But when we are gathered in the house—that is, in the assembly of the church—by the action of the Lord of hosts and by the power of the Spirit, he is present with us. We hear him in the gospel. Baptism and eucharist take us into his arms like children. We see him risen when our leaders follow him in serving and when the whole assembly welcomes those considered unimportant. So we welcome God. The second passion prediction, supported by Jeremiah and James, speaks reform to our assemblies: so that the gospel is always central, we gladly see the Risen One among us, our leaders serve, we all learn ways of mercy, and the heart of the meeting is open to the least.

SUNDAY, SEPTEMBER 25–OCTOBER 1
LECTIONARY 26, PROPER 21

Mark 9:38-50
Numbers 11:4-6, 10-16, 24-29
Psalm 19:7-14 The commandment of the LORD gives light to the eyes. (Ps. 19:8)
James 5:13-20

Having read these readings, consider this:

The gospel for today continues last Sunday's central Markan counsel for our assemblies, for our gatherings in "the house." Today that counsel is even sharper: do not enter into competition with other Christians; do not seek a centralized authority which you control; welcome gifts from others; do not hurt the faith of the marginalized; be ready to suffer persecution; and care about the preservation of the earth—work to preserve, just as salt preserves. These words may be heard as accusing us. So can the counsels of James: in our congregation, do we pray for each other, hear each other's confessions, gently tend to each other? Still, in the midst of our assemblies stands the one who did lose his hand and foot and eye—indeed, his life—to the persecutor. Jesus Christ, crucified and risen, is the true salt of the earth. He may speak these hard words, but he is himself the very presence among us of the mercy of God. In baptism, the fire of the Spirit that comes from him is poured out on us all, just as Moses anciently hoped. In eucharist we receive from him the "cup of water." We are brought by this gospel to be at peace with one another. Then we can begin again to enact what both Jesus in Mark and the author of James counsel. Then we may give up both the complaining and the envy narrated in Numbers. More: then we can live peacefully in the world as if this saying were really true: "Whoever is not against us is for us."

SUNDAY, OCTOBER 2–8
LECTIONARY 27, PROPER 22

Mark 10:2-16
Genesis 2:18-24
Psalm 8 You crown us with glory and honor. (Ps. 8:5)
Hebrews 1:1-4; 2:5-12

Having read these readings, consider this:

All of us have been touched by divorce, some of us are divorced, and none of us should find it easy to moralize amid these sorrows. All of us are afflicted with hardness of heart in one way or another. Using scripture to critique scripture, Jesus in Mark sets Genesis against Moses in Deuteronomy (24:1). He thereby both deepens the meaning of marriage and destabilizes marriage legalisms, rejecting any approved legitimacy in a man sending a woman away because he finds "something objectionable [or shameful] in her." But in the house—in the church, thus—Jesus recognizes that women, too, fail in marriage. In the church we all together know ourselves to be guilty. In the house he also welcomes and blesses the children, the little and marginalized ones. Today, in the house—in the assembly or in our own homes when we read the scripture—we see Jesus, who tasted death for us sinners. He is not ashamed to call us his dear family. By the power of the Spirit poured out from him, we are drawn to be the needy, undeserving children whom he blesses to receive the kingdom, to stand in the congregation with him before God. The marriage that will sustain and renew all of our marriages and all of our relationships with others is God's marriage with the earth. Because of Jesus Christ, God graciously says to us all, "This is truly flesh of my flesh!" The eucharist is the marriage banquet.

SUNDAY, OCTOBER 9–15
LECTIONARY 28, PROPER 23

Mark 10:17-31
Amos 5:6-7, 10-15
Psalm 90:12-17 So teach us to number our days that we may apply our hearts to wisdom. (Ps. 90:12)
Hebrews 4:12-16

Having read these readings, consider this:

Jesus' saying in Mark is quite serious; he means a *camel* and a *needle*. So the question of the disciples is also serious: "Then who can be saved?" If a relatively decent and religiously observant rich man cannot, then the implied answer is "No one." Certainly not us: we have not kept all the commandments since our youth, and we have not given all our possessions to the poor. Amos heightens the critique: we have not done public justice in an aching world. These words pierce us like a sword and lay us bare before the eternal judge. How shall we enter the kingdom of God? "For mortals it is impossible, but not for God." Blessed be this God that Jesus also looks at *us* and loves *us*. Or to say the matter with the Letter to the Hebrews, we have a high priest who is able to sympathize with our weaknesses. He is the one who, in his death, has given away all. In the risen Christ, we may come before God and find mercy and grace. More: in the church, though undeserving, we already now have one-hundredfold, sisters and brothers and mothers and children. We already, in the assemblies gathered into Christ by the Spirit, have one-hundredfold houses. In God's beloved world we already have one-hundredfold fields. To our astonishment, we are already on the other side of the eye of the needle. Beginning again to do justice and to share what we have with the poor, let us live like that is so!

SUNDAY, OCTOBER 16–22
LECTIONARY 29, PROPER 24

Mark 10:35-45
Isaiah 53:4-12
Psalm 91:9-16 You have made the LORD your refuge, and the Most High your habitation. (Ps. 91:9)
Hebrews 5:1-10

Having read these readings, consider this:

In Mark, the three "passion predictions" always come paired with words about discipleship: the first, on taking up the cross; the second, on serving and welcoming the child in the assembly; the third, on sharing Jesus' baptism and cup. Today's gospel comprises the words that follow the third prediction. Let those words convict us. We, too, often seek to be first, often support those who domineer in our society, or do the domineering ourselves. We are asked to give that up. While baptism and cup are gracious events in the assembly, they are also metaphors for Jesus' death. Jesus invites us to participate in them in both senses. Of course, the places at his right and left are not for us; they were prepared for the two thieves: as the old servant song said, "He was numbered with the transgressors." But baptism and cup *are* for us. In his death, given to us in both, are the wounds that heal us and make us whole. "The many"—the crowd, all the people, including us—are made righteous in the one who serves them and gives his life. He is a priest like Melchizedek—mysterious, not making offerings in any temple, but giving himself, and like Melchizedek, blessing God and us over bread and cup. Made offspring of the Servant by the Spirit, we are to be what we have received: also giving ourselves away in service.

SUNDAY, OCTOBER 23–29
LECTIONARY 30, PROPER 25

Mark 10:46-52
Jeremiah 31:7-9
Psalm 126 Those who sowed with tears will reap with songs of joy. (Ps. 126:5)
Hebrews 7:23-28

Having read these readings, consider this:

The *Timaeus*, a dialogue written by Plato, was one of the most widely known books in the ancient world. Its principal speaker, named Timaeus, is presented as a ruler and a philosopher of the Greek city of Locri in what is today southern Italy. One principal theme of the book is the praise of *sight* as the source of philosophy and ethics, including a throwaway, dismissive comment about anyone who is blind. Mark then strikingly pictures a descendent of this philosopher as a blind beggar silenced by the crowd. Let the text question us: Has our own philosophy blinded us? Or do we silence or dismiss people in need, including the exiles of our time? The son of Timaeus, who comes with weeping, is drawn with consolations by the Son of David. The philosopher's descendent names Jesus as his teacher. He comes to see. And with that gift, he follows Jesus into the story of the cross, the story of the once-for-all self-giving that saves us all. The Spirit enlivening this richly symbolic account draws us to join BarTimaeus. The gospel of Jesus our teacher can show us the way. Our baptismal immersion into Christ's death can bring us to see clearly. We *taste* the eucharist *and*, as if for the first time, *see* the goodness of God and God's world. Then, that God joins us to those in need, forming us to cry out with them for justice and for life.

SUNDAY, OCTOBER 30–NOVEMBER 5
LECTIONARY 31, PROPER 26

Mark 12:28-34
Deuteronomy 6:1-9
Psalm 119:1-8 Happy are they who seek the LORD with all their hearts. (Ps. 119:2)
Hebrews 9:11-14

Having read these readings, consider this:

"*This* is the commandment," says Moses introducing the *Shema*, its call to love God with all our being, and the necessity of binding this word onto all the occasions of life. Asked about the first commandment, Jesus in Mark answers with that very *Shema* text. Only, he then, surprisingly, adds a second about love of neighbor, a word drawn from an obscure corner of the law in Leviticus 19:18. For Jesus, this too should be a word marking all our life. Putting those two commandments together as greater than all others was religiously revolutionary and, in Mark, the end of any further questions put to Jesus. Luther used the two to organize the two tables of the ten commandments and, in the Small Catechism, added positive action toward the neighbor to his interpretations. We use the two to confess our sins: "We have not loved you with our whole heart; we have not loved our neighbors as ourselves." The scribe who knew these two commandments to be more important than sacrifices was "not far" from the kingdom. But the kingdom itself brings the *end* of sacrifices, of "dead works." The One who teaches the two commandments gives himself in the Spirit to God and so to all neighbors, including us, washes us clean, and feeds us with the milk and honey of the eucharist. Thus forgiven, we may begin again to keep these reinterpreted commandments. In assembly, we are gathered into this worship of the living God: "'tis a delightful road" (ELW 772).

ALL SAINTS DAY (NOVEMBER 1) OR ALL SAINTS SUNDAY

John 11:32-44
Isaiah 25:6-9
Psalm 24 They shall receive blessing from the God of their salvation. (Ps. 24:5)
Revelation 21:1-6a

Having read these readings, consider this:

We know tears. And the world around us is filled with yet more tears, beyond our knowing. In observing this day, the church honors tears. Jesus Christ weeps with us as the story says he did with Mary and Martha. Tears are welcome as we remember our dead and as we remember the countless people who have died and whose lives are hidden in God—all the saints. But Christ not only weeps with us; he has died with us and is risen and present in our midst. In the word of his death and resurrection, God has begun to wipe away all tears and make all things new. Baptized into Christ's life, we ourselves have been unbound from the fear of death and let go. By the power of the Spirit, the meal the assembly shares is already the very promised feast of the end of death. Then, made newly alive by God's dwelling among us mortals, we are invited in turn to unbind our neighbors from fear and let them go.

SUNDAY, NOVEMBER 6–12
LECTIONARY 32, PROPER 27

Mark 12:38-44
1 Kings 17:8-16
Psalm 146 The Lord lifts up those who are bowed down. (Ps. 146:8)
Hebrews 9:24-28

Having read these readings, consider this:

Perhaps Jesus in Mark is praising this widow who gives everything she has. Or perhaps he is sharply criticizing the religious establishment that "devours widows' houses." Or both. After all, just two verses further on in the book, Jesus foretells the utter destruction of the house of the temple to which the poor widow is contributing her all. We need to ask ourselves if our religion hurts others like this, while being primarily about our own good reputation. And we need to ask ourselves if we give all we have from the heart. Still, the two widows of today's readings are to be seen as examples of the many hidden holy ones of God—all the unknown saints—images for God's sustaining mercy and for Christ's eternal gift. Even more, following those images, for us Jesus Christ himself is the one who gives all he has. He is the meal and oil, his cross the "couple of sticks." He bears the sins of the many—of all—and brings us with him into the house that lasts. His meal is bread for us in every famine. Then the Spirit poured out from him may form us to share our own food and support with all the hungry world, seeking to stop self-serving religion.

SUNDAY, NOVEMBER 13–19
LECTIONARY 33, PROPER 28

Mark 13:1-8
Daniel 12:1-3
Psalm 16 My heart is glad and my spirit rejoices; my body shall rest in hope. (Ps. 16:9)
Hebrews 10:11-25

Having read these readings, consider this:

Every November, before Advent begins, there is always at least one Sunday that considers the end of the world. This year, this is that Sunday. The apocalyptic language in Daniel coincides with the same kind of language in Mark. And both coincide with our own experience: a time of anguish, great buildings thrown down, wars and rumors of wars, peoples set against peoples, earthquakes, famines. In Mark, written after the temple had been destroyed, this is not prediction but current description. The same is true for us—the end of the world as we know it is always now. Thinking of that truth, we continually pray, as Jesus taught us, "Save us from the time of trial." God does indeed save us. Not only can we imagine that a great archangel draws near with protection, not only can we trust that our names are written in God's book, but the gospel says that God actually comes all the way into the time of anguish in the world, making it the birth-time of the kingdom. Mark's apocalypse immediately precedes the story of Christ's passion, the great event of destruction. Yet, risen, Christ is present to us when we meet together. We do not need to look anywhere else. With hearts and bodies made clean in baptism, we assemble to hear the Holy Spirit empower the new covenant again among us, making us witnesses to God's faithfulness and encouraging us to love and good deeds in the anguished world.

CHRIST THE KING
SUNDAY, NOVEMBER 20–26
LECTIONARY 34, PROPER 29

John 18:33-37
Daniel 7:9-10, 13-14
Psalm 93 Ever since the world began, your throne has been established. (Ps. 93:2)
Revelation 1:4b-8

Having read these readings, consider this:

In Daniel's apocalyptic vision, terrifying beasts have ruled the world, but the ancient God of the fiery throne judges the beasts and establishes instead the reign of "one like a human being." In the apocalyptic vision of the last book in the Bible, the terrors of Roman imperial rule are all around, but John the elder, inspired by Daniel, sees Jesus coming to reign. We also are surrounded by terrors. Against those terrors, Jesus is an utterly new sort of king. Pilate calls him "king" just before he pronounces the sentence of execution, and he then puts that title over the cross. Jesus neither accepts nor rejects the title. Rather, in his death he testifies to the truth, he loves us, and he frees us from our sins. In his resurrection, grace and peace come to us from the God of the fiery throne, from the Holy Spirit seen as the spirits who hold the churches before God, and from Jesus. By baptism, this Jesus makes us a people of priests for this one triune God, called, ourselves, to bear witness and to invite our neighbors also not to be afraid of the terrors. In our assembly, once again, the books are opened, and God's merciful and life-giving judgment is announced.

CHAPTER 5

Readings for Year C

FIRST SUNDAY OF ADVENT

Luke 21:25-36
Jeremiah 33:14-16
Psalm 25:1-10 To you, O Lord, I lift up my soul. (Ps. 25:1)
1 Thessalonians 3:9-13

Having read these readings, consider this:

Advent, the church's time of waiting, reminds us that all of life involves waiting. Christians, however, long not only for personal matters but also for widespread justice to be done, for a fruitful earth to be restored, and for all people to be safe. As the gospel today honestly says, in our time too, fear, foreboding, and "distress among nations" are everywhere around us. Still, for Christians such waiting is opened toward hope by the presence of God's promises. As the fig tree's leaves signal the coming of summer, as the darkness in the north signals the nearness of the solstice and the return of light, so the gospel calls us to see the need of our time as pointing toward God's promised mercy. This apocalyptic chapter in Luke immediately precedes the story of the killing of Jesus, and for Christians that story points toward what follows: the resurrection and the presence of Christ among us. He is the promised righteous branch of the tree of David, a ruler unlike any other. Standing before him, we are called to wait confidently for all of God's promises for justice. We may appropriately act out our waiting with our own work for justice. In the power of the Spirit in this difficult time, the face-to-face assembly around Jesus Christ becomes a place of thanksgiving to God and love for our neighbors. The name of that assembly can rightly be "The Lord is our righteousness."

SECOND SUNDAY OF ADVENT

Luke 3:1-6
Malachi 3:1-4
Luke 1:68-79 In the tender compassion of our God the dawn from on high will break upon us. (Luke 1:78)
Philippians 1:3-11

Having read these readings, consider this:

For us in Advent, John the Baptist is the voice of which Isaiah spoke, the messenger Malachi promises. Both voice and messenger say the same thing, the very meaning of Advent: God is coming, through whatever difficult ways, bringing salvation, returning exiles to home. That ancient hope still echoes in our songs and in our hearts. But can we endure that coming? And how can all flesh see it? We come to the assembly, where—as we wait for the day of Jesus Christ—we give thanks and pray for other Christians and for all the world. Here we encounter now the down payment on what we hope for, and by the forgiveness of God, we do endure it. Alive in that assembly is not only baptism for forgiveness, but more: baptism that brings us into Jesus Christ, who is the new temple. In him, the word of God comes to us, in our real history. In him, we are purified. By the power of the Spirit, the meal of the temple is here. In our assembly and in our lives, we must show forth to all the world the very salvation of God that is coming.

THIRD SUNDAY OF ADVENT

Luke 3:7-18
Zephaniah 3:14-20
Isaiah 12:2-6 In your midst is the Holy One of Israel. (Isa. 12:6)
Philippians 4:4-7

Having read these readings, consider this:

We need to listen to John the Baptist, our principal Advent preacher. Collectively, we are indeed a "brood of vipers," boasting of our identity as if that saves us, not bearing fruitful deeds that help the world, not adequately sharing food and clothing, not content with simple wages. But there is more to say. The "one who is more powerful" is indeed coming, with the Holy Spirit and with fire. And in a hidden way, he has already come. On the tree of the cross he shares the lot of those cut down by the ax and burned by the fire. He joins us in waiting for justice and peace in the world. And the Spirit he gives us is the Spirit of peace, confidence, and the end of fear, poured into our lives by baptism into his death and resurrection. Already now, the Holy One for whom we wait is in our midst, forgiving and restoring us, rejoicing over humanity and over the earth itself as well-married spouses rejoice in each other. With joy this Sunday—in the word we hear and in the holy communion—we may continue to draw water from the wells of this salvation. Then, rejoicing in such great gifts, we may begin again to bear the fruits for which John calls.

FOURTH SUNDAY OF ADVENT

Luke 1:39-55
Micah 5:2-5a
Psalm 80:1-7 Let your face shine upon us, and we shall be saved. (Ps. 80:7)
Hebrews 10:5-10

Having read these readings, consider this:

Only now does Advent turn our waiting toward Christmas: the salvation for which the world longs is found already in the Christ child born of Mary. In all three years the fourth Sunday has us read from the first part of the story of that birth—Matthew's account of Joseph's dream in year A, the Lukan annunciation to Mary in year B, and the story of the visitation in this year. Filled with the Holy Spirit, the two women praise the action of God in the coming of Jesus. We thus encounter the holy Trinity in their words. In this child, born of a woman in Bethlehem according to the stories, the face of God does shine on us so that we might be saved. With Hebrews and with Mary's song we may speak this mystery in yet other ways. In his birth, Jesus comes to do God's will; his body offered once for all brings about the end of all sacrifices. More: in Christ's coming, God's end-time reversals begin: the proud and the powerful are deposed, the lowly are lifted up, and the hungry are filled. For us, the body of Christ we receive in the eucharist is the very Bread that was born in Bethlehem, the "house of bread," as the name means.

NATIVITY OF OUR LORD
CHRISTMAS EVE AND CHRISTMAS DAY

See above, in chapter 1.

FIRST SUNDAY OF CHRISTMAS

Luke 2:41-52
1 Samuel 2:18-20, 26
Psalm 148 The splendor of the Lord is over earth and heaven. (Ps. 148:13)
Colossians 3:12-17

Having read these readings, consider this:

The gospel on this Christmas Sunday is the sole narrative in the New Testament about the childhood of Jesus. Like the young Samuel in the house of the Lord at Shiloh, the twelve-year-old Jesus of the story is in the temple at Jerusalem, and he is notable for his serious engagement with questions. That he is found there "after three days" reminds us that "after three days" the crucified Jesus encounters us as risen. We are in his Father's house whenever we gather with the assembly in his name. By the power of the Spirit, the risen Jesus is with us in the midst of and encouraging our questions. Then, with Mary, we treasure the word of Christ in our hearts. We teach each other, and together we sing and give thanks. We are clothed for ministry like Samuel, our garment being our baptism into Christ. With that garment come all the gifts of the Spirit: compassion, kindness, forgiveness, love, and the very peace of Christ. Merry Christmas!

SECOND SUNDAY OF CHRISTMAS

See above, in chapter 1.

EPIPHANY OF OUR LORD

See above, in chapter 1.

BAPTISM OF OUR LORD, FIRST SUNDAY AFTER EPIPHANY SUNDAY, JANUARY 7–13 LECTIONARY 1

Luke 3:15-17, 21-22
Isaiah 43:1-7
Psalm 29 The voice of the LORD is upon the waters. (Ps. 29:3)
Acts 8:14-17

Having read these readings, consider this:

This day comes as a Trinity Sunday in winter in the northern hemisphere, summing up and giving us anew all that we have heard in Advent, Christmas, and Epiphany, just as Trinity Sunday in summer sums up Lent, Easter, and Pentecost. The holy Trinity is revealed at the water: Jesus, the Son and the one who has come, is in the water with the people; the Spirit descends upon him; the voice of God comes from heaven. In the gospel book, this one who is hidden with the people in the water goes on finally to be hidden in the baptism of his cross, sharing human sorrow and death. But he is risen and present with us now. In our reading of these texts and in our assembly, the holy Trinity is revealed again: the water of the font is here; we have been gathered into Christ by our baptism; the Spirit, the presence of God, is given to us; the voice of God speaks here—in word and sacrament—calling us beloved children of God. We may trust that we are called by the Lord's name and accompanied by the triune God through fire and water. We may let fear go. We may also share with our fearful neighbors the very assurance and love we ourselves have been given.

SECOND SUNDAY AFTER EPIPHANY
SUNDAY, JANUARY 14–20
LECTIONARY 2

John 2:1-11
Isaiah 62:1-5
Psalm 36:5-10 We feast upon the abundance of your house, O Lord. (Ps. 36:8)
1 Corinthians 12:1-11

Having read these readings, consider this:

On the Second Sunday after Epiphany in all three years, we read from the Gospel according to John, a text that shows forth the identity of Jesus. This year we read the story of the wedding at Cana, a story in which Jesus manifests his glory to the disciples and to us. The original readers of the story would have recognized in it traits from the myth of Dionysus, a Greek god who appeared at parties incognito, made extraordinary amounts of wine flow, and thus brought about an ecstatic replacement for an old religion. Jesus also acts incognito here, replacing religious purification water with an overwhelming amount of the good wine. But this sign is not yet Jesus' "hour"; that hour will come, in this gospel, when he is "lifted up" on the cross. Then we encounter the "third day" of his resurrection in every Sunday assembly. The sign points there, where he makes the new wine of the Spirit abundantly available, replacing any religion of purification. This "wine" is the Spirit of gladness, the Spirit that enables us to confess Jesus as Lord and gives us many different gifts for the assembly's common good. In that Spirit, we are no longer Forsaken and Desolate, but God calls us My Delight, the earth itself being married to God. We must share this wine with others.

THIRD SUNDAY AFTER EPIPHANY
SUNDAY, JANUARY 21–27
LECTIONARY 3

Luke 4:14-21
Nehemiah 8:1-3, 5-6, 8-10
Psalm 19 The teaching of the Lord revives the soul. (Ps. 19:7)
1 Corinthians 12:12-31a

Having read these readings, consider this:

The readings today give us images for the Sunday assembly. We too—all who can hear with understanding—gather as one. We too worship God and cry out, "Amen. Amen." We hear the scriptures read and interpreted. And though listening may make us want to weep at our failures or at the beauty of what we hear, we turn to a meal of refreshment and joy, and we send food and help to those who have none. Most centrally, in the power of the Spirit and in the name of God, Jesus stands among us as the fulfillment of what we read and as the gift of the meal. This meeting is that one body into which we all have been baptized. Even when we cannot meet, we remember the assembly by reading the scriptures and sending help to the hungry.

FOURTH SUNDAY AFTER EPIPHANY *(if before Transfiguration)*
SUNDAY, JANUARY 28–FEBRUARY 3
LECTIONARY 4

Luke 4:21-30
Jeremiah 1:4-10
Psalm 71:1-6 From my mother's womb you have been my strength. (Ps. 71:6)
1 Corinthians 13:1-13

Having read these readings, consider this:

Like last Sunday, these readings continue to give us images for our assembly's meaning and practice, but now the images come as warnings. We can hear the word of God fulfilled in Jesus today, yet we may act as if it belongs to us, as if we owe no thanks for it. We can celebrate baptismal washing and eucharistic eating, yet we can forget that the biblical models of these sacraments were first given to outsiders. We can have all sorts of religious gifts and powers in our community, but without our patient communal love they come to nothing. Luke uses the story of Jesus in Nazareth in his gospel to give us a foreshadowing of the cross. In the cross, God knows our failure and sorrow—God knows us—and in the cross God establishes our forgiveness. Rejoicing that we are known, we may turn again to hearing God's life-giving word and to welcoming the outsider.

FIFTH SUNDAY AFTER EPIPHANY *(if before Transfiguration)* SUNDAY, FEBRUARY 4–10 LECTIONARY 5

Luke 5:1-11
Isaiah 6:1-8
Psalm 138 I will bow down toward your holy temple. (Ps. 138:2)
1 Corinthians 15:1-11

Having read these readings, consider this:

Isaiah, Paul, and Peter all encounter God's awesome glory, are forgiven and cleansed, and then are sent. The unclean Isaiah sees the Lord amid the features and rituals of the temple. The risen Christ appears also to Paul, the persecutor, the least of the apostles. And as if also in a resurrection appearance, the failed sinner Peter beholds Jesus as he makes available such a multitude of fish that it seems the promise of Ezekiel 47 is being fulfilled. According to these scriptures, God brings life and purposeful mission out of sin, failure, and death. The gospel—the proclamation of the death and resurrection of Jesus—is the preeminent example of this action of God. By the power of the Spirit, that gospel comes here, where we are assembled. We hear this word, encountering the risen Christ in all the scriptures. We too sing, "Holy, holy, holy." We are forgiven and made newly alive. In the communion, the coal from the altar touches our lips. And we are sent to our needy world.

SIXTH SUNDAY AFTER EPIPHANY *(if before Transfiguration)* SUNDAY, FEBRUARY 11–17 LECTIONARY 6, PROPER 1

Luke 6:17-26
Jeremiah 17:5-10
Psalm 1 They are like trees planted by streams of water. (Ps. 1:3)
1 Corinthians 15:12-20

Having read these readings consider this:

Although in Matthew the beatitudes are spoken on a mountain among the chosen disciples, in Luke they occur on the plain, among a diverse crowd of people all seeking healing and hope. Furthermore, what is largely spiritual in Matthew has been made quite physical in Luke: Jesus here speaks to "you poor" and "you who are hungry now." Any assembly that hears these words today is called to pay attention to actual poverty, hunger, weeping, and persecution in our world and to join the movement to give help. Woe to us if we do not. But power still comes out of the risen Jesus Christ to also heal us. Indeed, Christ has been raised from the dead and stands among us, on our plain, in our assembly of needy people. With Jeremiah, the blessing is especially given to those, rich and poor, who trust in the Lord, rather than in their own strength. For Christians, the tree planted by streams of water is the cross of the risen Christ, where he was among the poor and hungry and persecuted ones. The water of the cross flows in baptism; there we are joined to Christ and brought by the Holy Spirit to trust in God and so turn to give relief to others.

SEVENTH SUNDAY AFTER EPIPHANY *(if before Transfiguration)*
SUNDAY, FEBRUARY 18–24
LECTIONARY 7, PROPER 2

Luke 6:27-38
Genesis 45:3-11, 15
Psalm 37:1-11, 39-40 The lowly shall possess the land; they will delight in abundance of peace. (Ps. 37:11)
1 Corinthians 15:35-38, 42-50

Having read these readings, consider this:

Christians have seen in the story of Joseph an image of what they know in Jesus Christ. Thrown into a pit, sold, and imprisoned, Joseph was then raised up, both forgiving and feeding those who had wronged him. Jesus, betrayed and killed by humanity, has become for us the source of forgiveness and bread. He is the one who loves, blesses, gives, does not judge, forgives, and is merciful as his Father is merciful. Risen and among us, he is already the harvest from the seed that Paul is expecting. Forgiveness and bread from him are here for us. Gathered by the Holy Spirit, like the crowd to which Jesus is speaking in Luke, we are called to become what we have been given: sowing love where there is hatred, pardon where there is injury.

EIGHTH SUNDAY AFTER EPIPHANY *(if before Transfiguration)*
SUNDAY, FEBRUARY 25–MARCH 1
LECTIONARY 8, PROPER 3

Luke 6:39-49
Isaiah 55:10-13
Psalm 92:1-4, 12-15 The righteous shall flourish like a palm tree. (Ps. 92:12)
1 Corinthians 15:51-58

Having read these readings, consider this:

The readings are full of familiar metaphors for a faithful life: first clearing one's own eyes; building on the strong foundation; rejoicing in God's victory over death. They also have images for our unfaithfulness: ignoring what we have heard; having no foundation; bringing evil out of an evil heart; fooling ourselves about our own bad eyesight. But perhaps the most important image here is the tree. The word of God is able to make evergreens or fig trees out of thorns. That can be seen as the change of which Paul speaks, and it is happing already now. The word that brings about that change is the gospel of the victory of Jesus Christ: by God's acting, the cross of Jesus has become the very tree of life, and his resurrection has become God's everlasting sign. This word of God does not return empty. In Christ and by his Spirit, we thorns and bramble bushes have begun to bear good fruit to serve our neighbor.

TRANSFIGURATION OF OUR LORD
LAST SUNDAY AFTER EPIPHANY

Luke 9:28-36
Exodus 34:29-35
Psalm 99 Proclaim the greatness of the Lord; worship upon God's holy hill. (Ps. 99:9)
2 Corinthians 3:12—4:2

Having read these readings, consider this:

Christians have come to see that this passage of Paul can easily lead to anti-Semitism. We ought rather consider how, also for Christians, looking at even the reflected glory of God is dangerous. When we behold Christ in word and sacrament, what is it that dies in us? Only Luke recounts what Moses and Elijah were talking about with Jesus: "his departure"—that is, his death. Christians read this story, which feels like a resurrection account yet includes knowledge of Jesus' death, just before Lent, when we will go up to Holy Week and Easter to remember that death and to celebrate that resurrection. But every Sunday in our assembly we believe we encounter the crucified and risen Christ. In him we are invited to see the glory of God openly, without fear, though that sight may utterly change us. What Peter and John and James kept silent about is said openly here. The Spirit of God is transforming us into what we see and what we receive: the shining image of God's life-giving mercy for all the world.

ASH WEDNESDAY

See above, in chapter 2.

FIRST SUNDAY IN LENT

Luke 4:1-13
Deuteronomy 26:1-11
Psalm 91:1-2, 9-16 God will give the angels charge over you, to guard you in all your ways. (Ps. 91:11)
Romans 10:8b-13

Having read these readings, consider this:

At the beginning of Lent, we once again pray, as in the Lord's Prayer, "Save us from the time of trial." But if we are tested, we know that Jesus is with us, he having endured all temptations before us. Indeed, his testing, both in the wilderness and at the "opportune time" of the cross, was the very time of trial that Jewish people expected would precede the coming of the day of God. The day does come. According to the story, he survived the tests by living from the scriptures, but not by misusing them as the devil does. Though the bread of the promised land is a wonderful gift, it comes from God, and it is the word of this God that gives true life. Though the help of angels is promised in the psalm, God—not magic—is the source of that help. The day of God arrives through Jesus' humility, in his death and resurrection. By the very Spirit that filled Jesus, the word of that resurrection is near us, on our lips and in our hearts, even when we fail the tests. Baptized by the Spirit, we receive in assembly, in scriptures and in eucharist, the very bread of the word, and we begin again to go up to Easter to celebrate the resurrection.

SECOND SUNDAY IN LENT

Luke 13:31-35
Genesis 15:1-12, 17-18
Psalm 27 In the day of trouble, God will give me shelter. (Ps. 27:5)
Philippians 3:17—4:1

Having read these readings, consider this:

Here are many images for our own days of trouble: Abraham has no children and no home; there are people who want nothing to do with the sufferings of Christ; leaders act like hungry foxes wanting to kill the mother hen; and a city seeks to stone those sent to it. But undeterred, Jesus is traveling—on the way toward Jerusalem, toward the cross, toward the third day of resurrection, and finally toward being present in our own assemblies, where we welcome him, singing, "Blessed is he who comes in the name of the Lord." In Lent, we remember that baptism gathers us under his wings, giving us citizenship together with him, making us children who join Abraham in trusting God's promises. Here, then, are also images of salvation. In Jesus Christ, who takes the place of the cut animals, the mystery of God makes a covenant with us, giving us not a land but shelter, life, hope, and the outpoured Holy Spirit. We may invite the violent city and the fearful people who have no home to take shelter in Christ with us.

THIRD SUNDAY IN LENT

Luke 13:1-9
Isaiah 55:1-9
Psalm 63:1-8 O God, eagerly I seek you; my soul thirsts for you. (Ps. 63:1)
1 Corinthians 10:1-13

Having read these readings, consider this:

All of us are the unfruitful tree. All of us deserve the fate of those Galileans. But Jesus is himself the gardener: we have another year. Lent calls us to repentance and new resolve. "Let the wicked forsake their way." And "do not become idolaters" and "do not complain, as some of them did." But there is yet more to say: God invites us to return to the waters of baptism, to come to the reliable word of mercy, and to eat and drink the gracious meal "without money and without price." Because Jesus Christ himself shared the lot of those Galileans, the Spirit poured out from his death and resurrection calls us to be among those nations who now run to God's abundant pardon. "Listen, so that you may live." Living by that Spirit, we will bring forth fruits of love.

FOURTH SUNDAY IN LENT

Luke 15:1-3, 11b-32
Joshua 5:9-12
Psalm 32 Be glad, you righteous, and rejoice in the LORD. (Ps. 32:11)
2 Corinthians 5:16-21

Having read these readings, consider this:

These readings give us words for Lent. At one time or another, we are all each brother, the wasteful, friendless, and despairing sinner and the self-righteous judge of others. In Lent we are invited to repent, to cry out for mercy, to return to the Lord our God. But every Sunday, Easter runs out to us before we have even finished Lent. Sunday itself, the weekly feast of the resurrection, is for us like Gilgal: having crossed the Jordan, the Israelites at the stone circle called Gilgal knew that their disgrace had been rolled away; they ate from the land. On Sunday, in the Spirit and because of Christ, God clothes us anew with our baptism and brings us to the feast of the new creation. Christ, "made to be sin" with us, has been in every pigsty, has shared the lot of those to whom no one gives anything. Risen, Jesus Christ is himself the robe and ring that the Father puts on us. And Jesus Christ is the feast of mercy to which the Father also invites us when we act like the older son. "This fellow welcomes sinners and eats with them." And indeed, "happy are they whose transgressions are forgiven and whose sin is put away."

FIFTH SUNDAY IN LENT

John 12:1-8
Isaiah 43:16-21
Psalm 126 Those who sowed with tears will reap with songs of joy. (Ps. 126:5)
Philippians 3:4b-14

Having read these readings, consider this:

We are close now to Holy Week and Easter, where the great new thing of God will be celebrated. Biblical "new things" are always a surprising reworking of the old: the God who made a way through the sea for people to escape slavery now makes a way through the wilderness, watering it, for those in exile to come home. That water flows to us in our baptism. So does the anointing oil of Mary. The old anointing of priests and kings now becomes the burial preparation of Jesus, for his cross was where he was shown forth as true priest and king for us. In John's gospel, the Passover is on Saturday (see 19:31), so the meal at Bethany, the first gathering with Jesus in a house reported in the fourth gospel, is held on Sunday. And this Sunday gathering becomes a foreshadowing of all the Sunday gatherings, narrated in John 20 and then continued in the church. When we gather on Sunday, our houses are filled by the Spirit with the fragrance of Jesus' resurrection. We are then sent to care for the poor whom we always have with us. In such Sunday assemblies and in such mission, we know Christ, the power of his resurrection, and the sharing of his sufferings.

SUNDAY OF THE PASSION, PALM SUNDAY

See above, in chapter 2.

THE THREE DAYS
MAUNDY THURSDAY, GOOD FRIDAY, VIGIL OF EASTER

See above, in chapter 2.

RESURRECTION OF OUR LORD, EASTER DAY

Luke 24:1-12
Isaiah 65:17-25
Psalm 118:1-2, 14-24 This is the day that the LORD has made; let us rejoice and be glad in it. (Ps. 118:24)
Acts 10:34-43

Having read these readings, consider this:

Isaiah's vision of a new heaven and a new earth is almost painful to read in our times: we know too many cries of distress; refugees routinely build houses and then are driven away; many children are born for calamity. But this day proclaims that Christ is risen, trampling down all death by his death. We may, like the apostles, regard that as an idle tale. Or like the many women of this gospel, we may trust this proclamation with our lives. The resurrection of Jesus is a down payment on Isaiah's vision, and we are therefore invited to live in our world unafraid, at peace, with deep respect for the old and the young, for the wolf and the lamb, for the city and the vineyard, as if the realization of the vision already surrounded us. Luke does not tell us the mechanics of the resurrection. Rather, the community comes to know its truth much as we do every Sunday: in the forgiveness of sins that comes also to us, in the witness of prophets and evangelists, and in eating and drinking with Jesus. In the power of the Spirit and because of the resurrection, our days now shall be like the days of a tree on God's holy mountain.

SECOND SUNDAY OF EASTER

John 20:19-31
Acts 5:27-32
Psalm 118:14-29 You are my God, and I will exalt you. (Ps. 118:28)
Revelation 1:4-8

Having read these readings, consider this:

The gospel shows us what is meant to happen in the Christian assembly: its people meet on Sunday, receive the Spirit poured out from Christ's death and resurrection, forgive sins, greet one another in peace, touch the wounds of Christ in holy communion, and come to believe again in the life-giving resurrection through the signs recounted in the gospel book. Because of the Holy Spirit, we who gather are made witnesses together with Peter and the apostles. In the holy Trinity, as the writer of the Revelation states, we are now all together priests before God for the sake of the life of the world. Blessed are those who have not seen and yet have come to believe.

THIRD SUNDAY OF EASTER

John 21:1-19
Acts 9:1-6
Psalm 30 You have turned my wailing into dancing. (Ps. 30:11)
Revelation 5:11-14

Having read these readings, consider this:

Sometimes a fish is only a fish: not here. In this second conclusion to the fourth gospel, fishing is a symbol for the work of the apostles sent in mission, successful only under the blessing of the risen Christ. More: the fish is a symbol of the chaos of the sea turned into food. Jesus does not wait for the disciples' catch; he already has the fish and bread to give away, signs of his death now made into life-giving food (see *ELW*, p. 89). In all of these readings the risen Christ is seen: by the writer of the Revelation, as the slaughtered Lamb at the center of all creation's praise; by Saul, as a blinding light who turns Saul into the great missionary theologian Paul; and by the disciples, as the giver of bread and fish who heals Peter from his denials. When we read these readings and when we gather in assembly, we too see the risen Christ. In the Spirit we sing to God and to the Lamb. We eat from the life-giving table. We are sent to bring God's healing name and death-destroying food into all the world.

FOURTH SUNDAY OF EASTER

John 10:22-30
Acts 9:36-43
Psalm 23 The LORD is my shepherd; I shall not be in want. (Ps. 23:1)
Revelation 7:9-17

Having read these readings, consider this:

Every year on the Fourth Sunday of Easter we celebrate the crucified and risen Jesus Christ as the good shepherd. Our texts today are full of paradoxes that proclaim this truth: the *slain Lamb* is the Shepherd of the great multitude; the blood of that Lamb washes their robes white; the *wounded hand* of the Risen One, which is the very hand of God, holds them in safety. All of these images show the cross as source of life also for us. As if our assembly were a flock of sheep, we together hear the voice of this Shepherd who knows us, speaking in the scriptures. In the power of the Spirit, we are led to the water of life that is baptism. In holy communion, a table is set before us. And like Tabitha, we are given renewed life—eternal life—and are turned toward the needs of the poor. But be careful: the first-century controversy between Christians and Jewish religious authorities, reflected in the gospel, ought not be projected into our times. And the raising of Tabitha, like the "Talitha" of Mark 5:41, is an *image* for our renewal, not an exact prescription for dealing with the dead. Our Shepherd causes us to stand and live, unafraid, now.

FIFTH SUNDAY OF EASTER

John 13:31-35
Acts 11:1-18
Psalm 148 The splendor of the LORD is over earth and heaven. (Ps. 148:13)
Revelation 21:1-6

Having read these readings, consider this:

In the fourth gospel, signs are frequently paired with discourses, both expressing in tandem the meaning of Jesus Christ. In the last part of the gospel, the great sign of the death and resurrection of Jesus is paired with the farewell discourse, chapters 13–17, the final way this gospel expresses the meaning of that death and resurrection. On the fifth, sixth, and seventh Sundays of Easter each year, we read from those chapters. According to this gospel, then, Judas acting to betray is the beginning of Jesus being glorified, and that glory is his cross-death, the sign of his love, and the source for a loving community. The other readings today surround this assertion, showing us more images of that community: early Christians learn not to make distinctions between people, and to this day our assemblies are places where we begin to see God dwelling in the midst of us, wiping away tears and starting to make all things new. Easter invites us to witness to the resurrection by mutual love and by trusting God to create the new in our world.

SIXTH SUNDAY OF EASTER

John 14:23-29
Acts 16:9-15
Psalm 67 Let the nations be glad and sing for joy. (Ps. 67:4)
Revelation 21:10, 22—22:5

Having read these readings, consider this:

Because of the resurrection of Jesus Christ, as we hear these texts and especially as we gather with Christ's people, we are already beginning to be in that city now. In the word, the Father and the Son come to make their home in us, and the Spirit reminds us of all that Jesus has said. In baptism, the water of life flows; our place of prayer is beside that river. In the eucharist we eat the fruits of the tree of life and find the healing leaves of that tree applied to us. All peoples and all their cultural gifts must be welcome here. There is no temple—no place for giving to God and for God to have a home—because here the triune God is giving to us and dwelling with us. We gladly join with a powerful woman and all her household in finding ourselves coming to Christian faith again. Christ is risen. "Do not let your hearts be troubled, and do not let them be afraid."

ASCENSION OF OUR LORD, THE FORTIETH DAY OF EASTER

See above, in chapter 2.

SEVENTH SUNDAY OF EASTER

John 17:20-26
Acts 16:16-34
Psalm 97 Rejoice in the Lord, you righteous. (Ps. 97:12)
Revelation 22:12-14, 16-17, 20-21

Having read these readings, consider this:

With the jailer and his household in this lively story, we too have been baptized and have joined the community of faith. In the image of the Revelation to John, we too have washed our robes in the blood of the Lamb. We too are among those who have believed through the word of Jesus' followers, the ones for whom the narrative says Jesus now prays. And we need this prayer. May we indeed be united so that the world will also believe. May we know that this unity comes because, in the Spirit, the Father and the Son come to dwell among us. The glory of Christ that we are to be given is God's own act of gracious giving. In assembly, we begin to gather where Christ is coming with this glory. We begin to enter already now through the gates of the promised city. In word and sacrament, we have access to the tree of life. In the Spirit this assembly, married as it is to the Lamb, cries out, "Come, Lord Jesus!" Jesus does come, and because of that coming, the water of life is available to everyone who is thirsty. Such stunning images!

DAY OF PENTECOST, THE FIFTIETH DAY OF EASTER

John 14:8-17, 25-27
Acts 2:1-21
Psalm 104:24-34, 35b Send forth your Spirit and renew the face of the earth. (Ps. 104:30)
Romans 8:14-17

Having read these readings, consider this:

How do we know that the spirit of a group in a room or the spirit that inspires us personally is the Spirit of God and not some other, perhaps destructive spirit? The Gospel according to John answers that the Spirit poured out from God comes to us because of the death and resurrection of Jesus and bears witness to him. As we gather in assembly on this fiftieth day of Easter, the Spirit enables us to pray to the Father in the name of Jesus and thus to know God and to know that we are children of God and heirs with the risen Christ. The Spirit gathers us, through scripture, sacrament, and prayer, into the very life of the holy Trinity. That Spirit is given to all flesh—people of all languages and classes, all ages and genders. Indeed, as the psalm says, the Spirit is intended to renew the life of all creatures and of the earth itself. Formed by this gift, let us follow the Spirit into concrete acts of earth-care.

THE HOLY TRINITY
FIRST SUNDAY AFTER PENTECOST

John 16:12-15
Proverbs 8:1-4, 22-31
Psalm 8 Your glory is chanted above the heavens. (Ps. 8:2)
Romans 5:1-5

Having read these readings, consider this:

Trinity Sunday sums up all we have heard of God's love in Lent and Easter and helps us see that God pours that love into our hearts by the Holy Spirit. By such love, our sufferings are transformed by hope. Three scriptural images for the Trinity are given here. In John, we continue to read from the farewell discourse as we did on many Sundays of Easter in this year C, and we hear of the Spirit who declares to us the things of Christ, which are also the things of the Father. The truth of the Trinity enfolds us. According to Paul, we stand before God because of Christ, and so the Spirit is poured out in us. The love of the Trinity saves us. In Proverbs, Christians see Woman Wisdom, the master worker beside the Lord in the creation of all things, as an image for Christ. For us, the Son of God was not created but was with God, being God's creative Word from eternity. Jesus Christ is our Woman Wisdom. The Trinity takes delight in all the world, including us. We can join God's wisdom in also taking delight in the creation. Thus, we are held within the life of the holy Trinity.

SUNDAY, MAY 24–28 *(if after Holy Trinity)*
LECTIONARY 8, PROPER 3

See above, at Eighth Sunday after Epiphany, February 25–March 1.

SUNDAY, MAY 29–JUNE 4 *(if after Holy Trinity)*
LECTIONARY 9, PROPER 4

Luke 7:1-10
1 Kings 8:22-23, 41-43
Psalm 96:1-9 Declare the glory of the LORD among the nations. (Ps. 96:3)
Galatians 1:1-12

Having read these readings, consider this:

The Gospel according to Luke, originally written for Gentiles, presents a Roman centurion positively as a man who has built an assembly-house, a synagogue, for the Jews. This centurion is a man of considerable authority, yet while he begs Jesus for help, he refuses to command Jesus to come into his house. In 1 Kings, as part of the dedicatory prayer for the temple, Solomon, in the presence of the whole assembly of Israel, asks that if foreigners pray "toward this house" for the name of the Lord, they will be heard. It is as if the centurion is such a foreigner and Jesus himself is the house toward which he prays. The centurion is indeed heard. We are also such foreigners in need. If we listen to Paul, who is writing to all the assemblies—the "churches"—in Galatia, but also to our assembly, we will not desert the gospel, the good news that the grace and peace of the triune God are for all people, including us and all foreigners. "Assembly" and "house" are everywhere in these readings. Our assembly will be a house for God's saving name when, by the power of the Spirit, the gospel of the risen Christ is there in word and sacrament.

SUNDAY, JUNE 5–11 *(if after Holy Trinity)*
LECTIONARY 10, PROPER 5

Luke 7:11-17
1 Kings 17:17-24
Psalm 30 My God, I cried out to you, and you restored me to health. (Ps. 30:2)
Galatians 1:11-24

Having read these readings, consider this:

Like Elijah the prophet, Jesus in this story has compassion on a destitute widow and raises her son from death. This story occurs only in Luke's gospel, but one chapter further on, in 8:40-56, the gospel narrates a story first found in Mark: Jesus raises a twelve-year-old girl. Jesus, who already embodies the last day, uses essentially the same words in both stories, symbolizing the final resurrection: "I say to you, get up!" As with Elijah, the word in his mouth is truth. Then to show that he is alive, the young man speaks. Similarly, the girl eats (8:55). In the mercy of God and by the power of the Spirit amid our misery and death, Jesus comes here where we read these words. As with Paul, the risen Christ is revealed among us, in the gospel saying now to us, "Get up!" The resurrection comes to us now. In assembly, we too speak—in scripture and song and prayer—and we too eat—in the holy eucharist. Christ has been given to us to make us alive. Then we should be given to our neighbors in need, to help more of the world say with the psalmist, "You have turned my wailing into dancing."

SUNDAY, JUNE 12–18 *(if after Holy Trinity)*
LECTIONARY 11, PROPER 6

Luke 7:36—8:3
2 Samuel 11:26—12:10, 13-15
Psalm 32 Then you forgave me the guilt of my sin. (Ps. 32:5)
Galatians 2:15-21

Having read these readings, consider this:

In the narratives of the gospels, Jesus—who is called "Christ," meaning "the anointed one"—is literally anointed only in this story and its parallels. In Mark, Matthew, and John, Jesus is anointed by a woman "beforehand for . . . burial" (Mark 14:8); he is the anointed Messiah for us in his death on the cross. In Luke, Jesus is anointed by a "woman in the city, . . . a sinner"; the anointed Messiah forgives sins. We hear, in these readings, of both a sinful monarch and a sinful unknown woman. The narratives leave room for us: we too are sinners in need of forgiveness. And Paul tells us of the source of that forgiveness—not works that try to prove our righteousness to God, but trust in God's grace in Christ. In the readings and in the assembly, we encounter and, at table, eat and drink that grace. But be careful with these readings: In spite of a long-mistaken biblical interpretation, Mary Magdalene of Luke 8:2 is not the same as this anointing woman of 7:37. Rather, Mary is one of several women with independent means who use their resources to help the disciples. Forgiven and healed in Christ, we should join all these women in acknowledging Jesus as our Messiah and in providing for others.

SUNDAY, JUNE 19–25 *(if after Holy Trinity)*
LECTIONARY 12, PROPER 7

Luke 8:26-39
Isaiah 65:1-9
Psalm 22:19-28 In the midst of the assembly I will praise you. (Ps. 22:22)
Galatians 3:23-29

Having read these readings, consider this:

In the last part of Isaiah, "Third Isaiah," God stands ready to welcome the people with open hands. But they turn away to their own devices, immersed in foul practices and a cult of death, divided from each other by the proclamation "Keep to yourself." We are that people. We can also find an image for ourselves in the man with mental illness living alone among tombs, bound with chains, and refusing to welcome Jesus. We, too, are oppressed by legions of sorrows and, sometimes, by legions of actual soldiers. But the story shows the man at last released, healed, and sitting "clothed and in his right mind" at Jesus' feet. Baptism has clothed us with Christ. In these readings and in the assembly, we sit at Jesus' feet. By the Spirit poured out here, God does welcome us. And far from being alone, we are all one in Christ, with distinctions of ethnicity, social status, and gender set aside. May it be so. In the midst of such an assembly, may we indeed praise the God of grace.

SUNDAY, JUNE 26–JULY 2
LECTIONARY 13, PROPER 8

Luke 9:51-62
1 Kings 19:15-16, 19-21
Psalm 16 I have set the LORD always before me. (Ps. 16:8)
Galatians 5:1, 13-25

Having read the readings, consider this:

We begin now to read from the central and most unique part of the Gospel according to Luke, the "travel narrative" (9:51—19:28), which we will read for nineteen Sundays. Jesus turns to travel toward Jerusalem, where he will be "taken up"—that is, where his death, resurrection, and ascension will take place. We are given the freedom to follow, as Elisha followed Elijah. That way of following will be "the path of life," as Psalm 16 says. But contrasting responses are imaged in the readings. We might instead follow the works of the "flesh"—that is, works of the self turned in on itself, protecting only itself. We might refuse to welcome Christ, as the Samaritans did. Or we might wish to destroy unbelievers as James and John do. Such is not the Spirit of Christ. As the alternate reading of Luke 9:56 says, "The Son of Man did not come to destroy the lives of human beings but to save them." In baptism, the Spirit of God is poured out on us from the death and resurrection of Jesus, saving us and forming us in the very freedom and generosity toward others that we see in Elisha giving away the oxen, that we see even more in Jesus Christ giving away himself. In such freedom, God will be our portion and our cup, "a rich inheritance."

SUNDAY, JULY 3–9
LECTIONARY 14, PROPER 9

Luke 10:1-11, 16-20
Isaiah 66:10-14
Psalm 66:1-9 All the earth bows down before you and sings out your name. (Ps. 66:4)
Galatians 6:7-16

Having read these readings, consider this:

Jesus continues on his way in the "travel narrative," and he sends a large number of disciples before him, with his authority and in his name. This story—which is more about the time of the church and our own time than it is about the time of the historical Jesus—now comes to us. We are often the ones who do not receive God's gift of peace. When we cleave to the new creation in Christ, however—when we receive the Spirit's gift in faith rather than try to prove ourselves with our religious observance—Paul speaks the blessing of peace and mercy on us. That peace comes because of the crucified and risen Christ. In the Spirit poured out from him, we are baptized and so made to be as God's city, drawn from all nations. In that same Spirit, we eat and drink in the eucharist and so drink from God as from a mother. Then we are made part of the seventy. We are invited to bear witness to God's peace and mercy in all our towns and cities, and to do so in simplicity and vulnerability, in the world as Christ is, without power, like a lamb amid wolves.

SUNDAY, JULY 10–16
LECTIONARY 15, PROPER 10

Luke 10:25-37
Deuteronomy 30:9-14
Psalm 25:1-10 Show me your ways, O Lord, and teach me your paths. (Ps. 25:4)
Colossians 1:1-14

Having read these readings, consider this:

The well-known parable of this Sunday's gospel gives us a story about dangerous travel located within the "travel narrative" of Luke. We may rightly ask ourselves whether we are the religious people who "pass by on the other side" to avoid the wounded in our world. The parable can accuse us. But we may also be the half-dead man in the ditch, afraid and alone. If so, then we hear of an outsider who comes to save us. For us, to whom the gospel, the word of truth, has come, the outsider who saves us is the crucified Christ. In the power of the Spirit, the Risen One bandages us and pours on oil and wine in the word and sacraments. Because of this grace and peace from the triune God, our assemblies can be an inn for our recovery. Give thanks for those churches and pray for them. Then we turn, to act toward our neighbors as Christ has acted toward us. That word about loving our neighbors is indeed not far away, across the sea or in heaven, but near to us. By the gift of the Spirit, it is in our mouths today and in our hearts.

SUNDAY, JULY 17–23
LECTIONARY 16, PROPER 11

Luke 10:38-42
Genesis 18:1-10a
Psalm 15 Lord, who may abide upon your holy hill? (Ps. 15:1)
Colossians 1:15-28

Having read these readings, consider this:

We are those who were hostile and estranged, doing evil deeds. And Jesus Christ, in the power of the Spirit and by his cross, has reconciled us and all things to God. We are refreshed in that reconciliation when, with Mary, we listen to the word and when, with Martha, we welcome Jesus and serve the meal to each other without being distracted by accusing others of not serving. Be careful here: this gospel is not about passivity being better than activity nor about silent listening as the best way for women. After all, Martha's necessary "tasks" are called *diakonia* in the Greek, the very word often used for "ministry" in the New Testament. No, the problem is the accusation, and this gospel is for us all. The meal in Martha's house is an image for our assembly. So is the abundant meal at Mamre. Christians take the visitors at the latter meal as an image for the presence of the triune God. Both meals are marked by hearing a word of promise, eating and drinking with God, and serving each other—exactly as in the best practice of our assembly. Listen to the promise of the Letter to the Colossians: the mystery that is now revealed means that the one in whom all things hold together—all things!—the one whose blood makes peace, is now in our assembly, among us, just as the Lord is at Mamre and the Lord Jesus is in the house.

SUNDAY, JULY 24–30
LECTIONARY 17, PROPER 12

Luke 11:1-13
Genesis 18:20-32
Psalm 138 Your steadfast love endures forever; do not abandon the works of your hands. (Ps. 138:8)
Colossians 2:6-15

Having read these readings, consider this:

The Lord's Prayer asks God about the coming day of the Lord, about the dawning "kingdom," and about being saved from the time of trial. But it also asks confidently for bread and forgiveness now, today, "each day." The community that makes this prayer—the "us" of the prayer—is the assembly that has been buried in baptism, forgiven, and made alive together with Christ by God who gives the Spirit; the community rooted like a tree and built up like a temple in Christ. Because that assembly can trust God to give the good gifts of the kingdom, it prays in confidence for the needy world, the world marked by outcries against injustice and corruption. Indeed, in its intercessions, the church can dare to beg God with persistence, like Abraham, asking for bread and forgiveness for everyone. This assembly is formed by receiving from God both forgiveness and the holy bread in its own meeting.

SUNDAY, JULY 31–AUGUST 6
LECTIONARY 18, PROPER 13

Luke 12:13-21
Ecclesiastes 1:2, 12-14; 2:18-23
Psalm 49:1-12 My mouth shall speak of wisdom. (Ps. 49:3)
Colossians 3:1-11

Having read these readings, consider this:

The first reading and the gospel today are particularly acute examples of biblical wisdom. The wise know that we all die; fools live as if there are no limits. We ourselves are frequently among the fools. But the Letter to the Colossians urges us not to lie to each other. We do indeed die. Storing up treasures for ourselves—"greed," as the letter says—counts as vanity and chasing after wind, and that vanity does become a source of our despair. Instead, Luke's gospel urges us to be "rich toward God." But what is that? The one who is truly rich toward God is the crucified and risen Jesus Christ. In baptism, we have been clothed in him and in the new self that comes from him, constantly renewed by his Spirit. In baptism, we have already died and our true life is hidden in him. We are to be where he is. Be careful here: this is not a way out of the limits but a transfiguration of our existence within limits. "Above" is a metaphor for God, and the right hand of God is everywhere. Where is Christ? With us in our limits; with the poor and suffering ones; in word and sacrament in the assembly; and moving us to open our barns toward the needs of our neighbors and of the earth itself. Let us set our minds there.

SUNDAY, AUGUST 7–13
LECTIONARY 19, PROPER 14

Luke 12:32-40
Genesis 15:1-6
Psalm 33:12-22 Let your lovingkindness be upon us, as we place our hope in you. (Ps. 33:22)
Hebrews 11:1-3, 8-16

Having read these readings, consider this:

"Do not be afraid," says the Lord to Abram in this Yahwist account in Genesis. "Do not be afraid," says Jesus to the "little flock" in the Gospel according to Luke. "Do not be afraid," says the liturgy to us today. Why not? Is not fear what we most expect from life in the world? That may be, but here we are turned toward what is unexpected. An old, childless couple, "as good as dead," has a child and then millions of descendants, including us. God gives the kingdom away to a "little flock," a flock that includes us. Our treasure is "in heaven" when it is given away as alms to the poor. And most surprising of all—surprising us like a thief in the night—when the master comes, he serves a meal to his own slaves—exactly as the risen Christ serves us in our assembly today. Christians believe that the marriage feast from which that "master" to us is coming is the cross and empty tomb of Christ through which God has been wed to the world. We come to trust all of this good news because of the faith that the Holy Spirit stirs up in us. So, little flock, do not be afraid.

SUNDAY, AUGUST 14–20
LECTIONARY 20, PROPER 15

Luke 12:49-56
Jeremiah 23:23-29
Psalm 82 Arise, O God, and rule the earth. (Ps. 82:8)
Hebrews 11:29—12:2

Having read these readings, consider this:

The Gospel according to Luke contains many stories full of mercy, but today this good word also comes with a critical edge, a burning fire. The gospel thereby speaks together with the rejected prophet Jeremiah and the great cloud of suffering witnesses to faith in the Letter to the Hebrews. Not all religion is good. It can instead be marked by our self-deluding dreams and, like the gods in today's psalm, an absence of care for the humble and needy of the earth. Religion can be straw rather than wheat. It can refuse to interpret honestly the sufferings of the present time. Jesus Christ takes on those sufferings. His death is the shame he endures, the cause of divisions among those who refuse the word of the cross, a word like a hammer. But his death is also the baptism through which he brings us to God and in which he becomes "the pioneer and perfecter of our faith." In the power of the Spirit, the word of his resurrection is saving fire in the midst of our assembly. In that assembly, he is the wheat that yields bread for our life. Baptism, word, and table make us also to be witnesses to the God who fills heaven and earth.

SUNDAY, AUGUST 21–27
LECTIONARY 21, PROPER 16

Luke 13:10-17
Isaiah 58:9b-14
Psalm 103:1-8 The Lord crowns you with mercy and steadfast love. (Ps. 103:4)
Hebrews 12:18-29

Having read these readings, consider this:

Sometimes pointing the finger at others and speaking evil of them seems to be what our religion is mostly about. The prophet calls us to stop. And the prophet calls us to keep a holy sabbath. In the gospel, Jesus keeps sabbath by enabling a bent-over woman to stand upright. We must not use this text to point the finger at the Jews. Christians need to know that sabbath among the Jews is a beautiful thing, a watered garden in time, a mostly domestic observance of holy rest. But what is it among us? For us to come to sabbath, to come to that rest, is to come into assembly around Jesus Christ risen. He has been bent-over in death with all of us bent-over ones, and now our fiery God has raised him up to stand among us. By the gift of the Spirit, our assemblies flow with the water of baptism and abound with the food of the eucharist to make us strong. The Risen One causes us to stand with him already now in an assembly that anticipates the city of God. For us, sabbath is not a day but that assembly. There we are formed to offer food and help to the hungry of the world and to care for creation itself, repairing breaches and restoring streets.

SUNDAY, AUGUST 28–SEPTEMBER 3
LECTIONARY 22, PROPER 17

Luke 14:1, 7-14
Proverbs 25:6-7
Psalm 112 The righteous are merciful and full of compassion. (Ps. 112:4)
Hebrews 13:1-8, 15-16

Having read these readings, consider this:

In the Gospel according to Luke, and especially in its "travel narrative," Jesus is frequently at a meal. This Sunday he speaks about behavior at meals, recommending extraordinary humility to guests and extraordinary hospitality to hosts, hospitality that welcomes the poor and the ordinarily uninvited. The gospel reading is a narrative elaboration of the passage from Proverbs. The reading from Hebrews can be read as a further elaboration: we are to show hospitality to strangers, as Abraham did to the three angels who were the very presence of God. More: at table we are to remember the imprisoned and the tortured. Whoever gives such a meal? We believe that Jesus does, here, in the assembly, where he welcomes us and all who come. Jesus himself was among the imprisoned and the tortured, and though he is the same yesterday, today, and forever, his self-gift here enables us to remember all those who suffer. By the Spirit which he pours out, we are brought to experience this meal as the metaphoric "sacrifice" that is well pleasing to God: here we give thanks through Christ; here we are formed to give to others as Christ does to us.

SUNDAY, SEPTEMBER 4–10
LECTIONARY 23, PROPER 18

Luke 14:25-33
Deuteronomy 30:15-20
Psalm 1 They are like trees planted by streams of water. (Ps. 1:3)
Philemon 1-21

Having read these readings, consider this:

Simply by hearing this story, we are among the large crowd that journeys with Jesus in the Lukan "travel narrative." But in spite of the counsel of Jesus, we frequently make bad decisions, turning away from God's blessing and refusing to count the cost of belonging to the kingdom. It is good for us to know that, for us, "choosing life" can mean trusting that there is forgiveness for us in Christ and holding fast to that promise of God. Jesus Christ is the one who has reliably carried the cross, cleaving to the company around him, cleaving to *us*, rather than to his own actual family or even his own life. In him we find the tree planted by streams of water. We are baptized in that water. Then, like Philemon, Apphia, and Onesimus, we are given a new family and a new chance at acting in the way of forgiveness and the way of the cross ourselves. Our assembly, like theirs, is called to transcend class, to love and to liberate each other, refreshed in Christ.

SUNDAY, SEPTEMBER 11–17
LECTIONARY 24, PROPER 19

Luke 15:1-10
Exodus 32:7-14
Psalm 51:1-10 Have mercy on me, O God, according to your steadfast love. (Ps. 51:1)
1 Timothy 1:12-17

Having read these readings, consider this:

The meals with which the Gospel according to Luke is full continue here: Jesus eats with sinners. Then he tells the stories of finding the lost and rejoicing. The final line of each story points to *God* rejoicing: "in heaven" and "before the angels." We can thus see *God* as the searching shepherd and the sweeping woman. Just so, God finds the lost people through Moses and finds the lost Paul through Christ. Still, the behavior of the searcher in the stories is strange: the shepherd leaves all the other sheep to search; the woman spends more than her single coin in throwing a party! And how does God search and sweep? In the strangeness of the cross of Christ, where lost humanity is sought exactly where it is lost, in death and the fear of death. Then, in the resurrection, we are the sheep that God carries and the coin that God holds. By the power of the Spirit, our assembly this Sunday is the rejoicing party; our eucharist is Jesus eating with sinners. The saying in the post-Pauline letter is indeed sure: Christ Jesus saves sinners, including us.

SUNDAY, SEPTEMBER 18–24
LECTIONARY 25, PROPER 20

Luke 16:1-13
Amos 8:4-7
Psalm 113 The Lord lifts up the poor from the ashes. (Ps. 113:7)
1 Timothy 2:1-7

Having read these readings, consider this:

The Pauline follower who wrote 1 Timothy here gives us the church's rule of prayer: pray for everyone. That rule of prayer then shows us the church's rule of faith: everyone is in need; everyone can be saved; God is gracious. And we see that grace especially in this: Christ gives himself away to ransom everyone and bring us all to God. Gathered around the giving Christ in the assembly, we too need to learn to give. Today's difficult and uniquely Lukan parable can call us into such giving. The true riches are not found in our protecting such money as we have but in turning with what we have to a needy world. May God keep us from trampling on the needy and cheating the poor. By this word, by the Spirit poured out on us in baptism, by our intercessions and collection for the poor in the assembly, and by the meal that feeds us all alike, may we be made children of the light and formed into practitioners of the generosity of Christ.

SUNDAY, SEPTEMBER 25–OCTOBER 1
LECTIONARY 26, PROPER 21

Luke 16:19-31
Amos 6:1a, 4-7
Psalm 146 The Lord gives justice to those who are oppressed. (Ps. 146:7)
1 Timothy 6:6-19

Having read these readings, consider this:

We have Moses and the prophets, but we also have the witness of one who has risen from the dead. Yet, too many of the poor still lie unheeded at our gates, while, like the people Amos accuses, most of us eat and drink richly. The parable in Luke is a metaphor for the great chasm that is fixed even now between the rich and the poor, and we are often on the wrong side of that chasm. What shall we do? At the very least, be grieved for the ruin of people's lives. But then, know that the Risen One who is in our midst has shared the lot of these ruined ones. By the power of the Spirit, his resurrection is the beginning of the healing of harms. His eucharist is a taste of cool water, a binding up of wounds, a place by Abraham's side. Then we may begin to follow him across the chasm, learning from him to be generous and ready to share. As Martin Luther wrote, having tasted this banquet of love, we must then feel with Christ "all the unjust suffering . . . with which the world is everywhere filled to overflowing." We "must fight, work, pray, and," at least, "have heartfelt sympathy" (*The Blessed Sacrament of the Body of Christ*, 9), thus fighting the good fight and seeking to avoid the love of money.

SUNDAY, OCTOBER 2–8
LECTIONARY 27, PROPER 22

Luke 17:5-10
Habakkuk 1:1-4; 2:1-4
Psalm 37:1-9 Commit your way to the LORD; put your trust in the LORD. (Ps. 37:5)
2 Timothy 1:1-14

Having read these readings, consider this:

The follower of Paul who wrote 2 Timothy invites us today to recover the gift of the Spirit: not cowardice, but a spirit that makes us strong, loving, and wise. But how? The texts today are at first discouraging: we do not have faith like a mustard seed; we look at a world full of violence, and God seems silent; and we do not join in suffering for the gospel. Wait for the vision, for the sign, says Habakkuk. What sign? We know from the rest of the gospel that the cross is like a mustard seed that becomes the tree of life (Luke 13:19) and that in the eucharist Christ does, surprisingly, come and serve us (12:37), even if "we are worthless slaves." Here is the sign: our Savior has abolished death and brought life to light through the gospel. We are made righteous, and we live by faith in that gift. With power and love and wisdom, we should make word and sacrament, the means that proclaim this sign, so large that they can be seen and trusted in this needy world.

SUNDAY, OCTOBER 9–15
LECTIONARY 28, PROPER 23

Luke 17:11-19
2 Kings 5:1-3, 7-15c
Psalm 111 I will give thanks to the LORD with my whole heart. (Ps. 111:1)
2 Timothy 2:8-15

Having read these readings, consider this:

We are often among the ungrateful, the ones continually helped and healed who do not give thanks. The Samaritan, an outsider, returns to give thanks to Jesus. But then, the Samaritan would not have been welcome in the Jerusalem temple. Coming as he does, he gives witness to what later Christians believe: Jesus Christ, who in the crucifixion was himself made an unclean outsider, is both our temple and our priest, giving welcome to outsiders and sinners. If we are faithless, he remains faithful. In the power of the Spirit, our thanksgiving to God in the assembly can be with and through Jesus Christ. Hearing this word, we are immersed in our baptism again and made clean like Naaman. Remembering Jesus Christ raised from the dead, we give thanks at the table again, with our whole heart. Having died with Christ, we are made alive with him.

SUNDAY, OCTOBER 16–22
LECTIONARY 29, PROPER 24

Luke 18:1-8
Genesis 32:22-31
Psalm 121 My help comes from the LORD, the maker of heaven and earth. (Ps. 121:2)
2 Timothy 3:14—4:5

Having read these readings, consider this:

Luke's gospel urges us, both here and in its reflections on the Lord's Prayer (11:5-8), to join those who persistently beg God for justice and help. We are to stand with a world full of "widows," with all those many whose unconsoled sufferings even now cry out to heaven. And we are to be like Jacob, wrestling with God: "I will not let you go unless you bless me." But the gospel, as it continues, makes clear that the one who most takes on that role is Jesus himself. In his cross he joins the lot of all the wretched of the earth. In the event of the cross he wrestles with God. But in the resurrection, God gives the blessing, and Christ's risen presence among us shows us God's down payment on justice for all people. The risen Christ himself will at last be the judge, the face of God's mercy. The sacred writings convince and encourage us to trust this word. Gathered in assembly by the Holy Spirit, we hear these scriptures, we once again join in persistent prayer for the needy world, we receive the blessing in the meal of Christ, and we are sent to stand with our neighbors as signs of hope.

SUNDAY, OCTOBER 23–29
LECTIONARY 30, PROPER 25

Luke 18:9-14
Jeremiah 14:7-10, 19-22
Psalm 84:1-7 Happy are the people whose strength is in you. (Ps. 84:5)
2 Timothy 4:6-8, 16-18

Having read these readings, consider this:

Politics, business, events between nations, and even our very families are too often marked by the destructive actions of people with concern only for themselves. So also, alas, is religion. The Pharisee in this Lukan story acts as if he owns the temple; this report of his religious practice may indeed be accurate. But his trust, as Jesus says, is in himself, and as some translations put it, his prayer is to himself as well. We need to hear the warning: our religious practice can be like this, marked by contempt for others. Let us join the publican and Jeremiah in confessing our sins and genuinely praying to God. The promise we can rely on is this: God is in our midst, and we are called by God's name. How is this so? Jesus Christ has shared the lot of those who long for forgiveness, and the Spirit has gathered us into his risen presence and into the very life of the triune God. Biblical religion is not about our accomplishments and pride but about this God's endless mercy. Witness to that mercy makes up the "good fight"—the fight for the gospel and against self-serving religion—of which a follower of Paul writes in 2 Timothy.

SUNDAY, OCTOBER 30–NOVEMBER 5
LECTIONARY 31, PROPER 26

Luke 19:1-10
Isaiah 1:10-18
Psalm 32:1-7 All the faithful will make their prayers to you in time of trouble. (Ps. 32:6)
2 Thessalonians 1:1-4, 11-12

Having read these readings, consider this:

The Lukan "travel narrative" now concludes "near Jerusalem" (19:11), in the house of Zacchaeus. And today salvation comes to our house—to our own homes, wherever we are reading these texts, but also especially to the "house" where we assemble as church. But our assemblies must not be the "solemn assemblies" that Isaiah reproaches; we must not do religious things if there is blood on our hands or if we have been defrauding our neighbors. Rather, let us confess our sins and begin again to seek justice. Because of the presence of Jesus Christ in our assembly's house, there is water here to wash us clean, a meal where Jesus is both guest and host, and an occasion to give to people in need. These things are what "salvation" looks like. Such an assembly will be—like the church of the Thessalonians—gathered by the Spirit into the holy Trinity. We may give thanks for all the assemblies of God, when they are like the gathering in the home of Zacchaeus, and pray that the Lord Jesus may be glorified in them.

ALL SAINTS DAY (NOVEMBER 1) OR ALL SAINTS SUNDAY

Luke 6:20-31
Daniel 7:1-3, 15-18
Psalm 149 Sing the LORD's praise in the assembly of the faithful. (Ps. 149:1)
Ephesians 1:11-23

Having read these readings, consider this:

In spite of whatever beasts arise seeking to rule the earth, the text in Daniel promises that the holy people of the Most High—the saints of God, the assembly of the faithful—will receive the kingdom. But when Christians read Daniel, they notice that, different from the beasts, the symbol for this people is "one like a human being," a Son of Man (Dan. 7:13). And Christians have believed that they know this Son of Man in Jesus Christ. Indeed, while all believers through the ages and now may be called the "holy people," thus "the saints," we also know that only one is holy. As the Gloria sings, "You alone are the Holy One . . . , Jesus Christ." In the cross, he was the one who was poor and hated. In the resurrection, he is above all rule and dominion. Yet he brings with himself, into the inheritance from God, all the poor and hungry, all those who in baptism have been sealed with the Holy Spirit, all those who hear the word of truth, all those who thus are part of the body of Christ. Receiving such a gift, we are to be indeed the holy people that God in Christ has made us, acting in love toward others.

SUNDAY, NOVEMBER 6–12
LECTIONARY 32, PROPER 27

Luke 20:27-38
Job 19:23-27a
Psalm 17:1-9 Keep me as the apple of your eye; hide me under the shadow of your wings. (Ps. 17:8)
2 Thessalonians 2:1-5, 13-17

Having read these readings, consider this:

In November we begin again to consider death, and these readings help us. First, however, they may accuse us: we may be the ones who engage in needless religious arguments or in exaggerations in any argument—like this extreme case of Levirate marriage—or in anxiety about life after death. But as the letter written most likely by a successor of Paul says, in the holy Trinity there is forgiveness, comfort, and good hope. Sanctified by the Spirit, we may stand firm on the rock who is Christ. On him, in his wounds, Job's hope and our own is already inscribed. In his risen presence with us now, we see God beside us as our redeemer. In him, in word and sacrament, we encounter the very burning bush. Jesus' answers make clear that, before God, a woman does not finally belong to anyone. Even more, the most important thing to say about life after death is a word about *God*, not about us. Because God is God of the living, life is with us now and we may trust God with our future. Let this word strengthen us in every good work.

SUNDAY, NOVEMBER 13–19
LECTIONARY 33, PROPER 28

Luke 21:5-19
Malachi 4:1-2a
Psalm 98 In righteousness will the Lord judge the world. (Ps. 98:9)
2 Thessalonians 3:6-13

Having read these readings, consider this:

We come now to Luke's version of the "little apocalypse," the words about the end of time largely shared with Mark and Matthew. We discover that these words can fit any time, including our own. With wars, persecutions, and natural disasters, we are always at the end of time, the day of judgment. But Christians believe that *God* is the judge, the sun that will both burn up evil and send out healing rays of light. In the midst of the turmoil of the world, as the apocalypse says, we ought not place ultimate trust in magnificent buildings, beautiful art, religious pretenders, governmental leaders, or even family values, but only in that healing sun. In the gospel, these words come just before the story of Jesus' passion. He is the one brought before rulers and put to death. In his cross, evil is already destroyed; in his resurrection, the sun of righteousness rises. That sun is with us in word and sacrament, forming us, even in difficult times, to endure, to do what is right, to work gladly for the good of the community, indeed to help support those who cannot work. The bread of the eucharist is given to us all.

CHRIST THE KING
SUNDAY, NOVEMBER 20–26
LECTIONARY 34, PROPER 29

Luke 23:33-43
Jeremiah 23:1-6
Psalm 46 I will be exalted among the nations. (Ps. 46:10)
Colossians 1:11-20

Having read these readings, consider this:

We come to the end of the church year, and we begin to turn to Advent by encountering this Sunday of the Reign of Christ. All three of the readings are full of references to kings: God will raise up a just and righteous king to replace the world's destructive rulers; God has transferred us into the kingdom of the beloved Son, in whom all things, including all rulers, have been created; and "King of the Jews" is written on Christ's cross. But then we see what an utterly new "king" this is. "King" is a word used to mock Jesus, not praise him; it is, indeed, the very trumped-up Roman charge for which he is being killed. All things created in him hold together and are brought to peace through the blood of his cross, not through any royal behavior on his part. And the wise justice he enacts is found in the forgiveness he offers his killers and in the welcome he gives the thief to his "kingdom." Jesus is king by being no king at all. These texts all criticize our authorities, calling them to a very different kind of power. By the work of the Spirit, as we read these readings and keep the holy supper, we are indeed transferred today to the realm where this mercy rules. Then we are invited to live with others the very mercy we have been given here.

CHAPTER 6

Readings for Lesser Festivals When Observed on Sunday

NAME OF JESUS, JANUARY 1

Luke 2:15-21
Numbers 6:22-27
Psalm 8 How majestic is your name in all the earth! (Ps. 8:1)
Galatians 4:4-7

Having read these readings, consider this:

Today is the eighth day of Christmas, and today, at the very beginning of a secular new year, we consider one small part of the Christmas proclamation: that Jesus was *named*, as any human being is named. But in this human being and in his risen presence now among us, the face of the eternal Lord of all shines on us. Indeed, in baptism this name has been put on us, and so we have been drawn into the life of the triune God: the Spirit from the Son has been put in our hearts so that we might stand before God and cry out, "Abba!" In this new year, with Mary, let us treasure that name and that Spirit in our hearts and let us, with the shepherds, make known to our world what we have seen God do.

PRESENTATION OF OUR LORD, FEBRUARY 2

Luke 2:22-40
Malachi 3:1-4
Psalm 84 How dear to me is your dwelling, O LORD. (Ps. 84:1)
Hebrews 2:14-18

Having read these readings, consider this:

According to Luke, the Lord whom we seek does indeed come to the temple, but in a surprising way: in this small child. The Lukan infancy narrative combines two temple rites: the purification of the mother from the uncleanness of childbirth, and the redemption of the firstborn male child. The parents bring the offering of the poor: two birds, to be killed in the stead of the child. But to a reader who knows the biblical tradition, the child himself is the Lamb (see Leviticus 12:6-8). And his death, the death that will destroy the power of death and reveal the inner thoughts of many, is only postponed. We join Simeon and Anna in beholding this event. In our assembly, we keep the word-service with Anna the prophet: we sing God's praises, we speak the promises for redemption, and we pray. Inspired by the Spirit, we also celebrate the holy supper with Simeon: we take the presence of Christ into our hands and we sing of the Light we thereby see. Now we too may go in peace. The Lord suddenly in the temple, the refiner's fire, the child, the Lamb, does purify our offerings, making them into thanksgiving and service to our neighbor.

JOHN THE BAPTIST, JUNE 24

Luke 1:57-80
Malachi 3:1-4
Psalm 141 My eyes are turned to you, Lord GOD. (Ps. 141:8)
Acts 13:13-26

Having read these readings, consider this:

We celebrate John the Baptist and his birth on a day close to the summer solstice, the longest of days in the northern hemisphere (for one old reason, see John 3:30). The Baptist, who has gone before the Lord to prepare the way, is called the greatest of those born of women (Matthew 11:11; Luke 7:28), yet John is not the Light. By the mercy of God, the true Light, the "dawn from on high" that gives light to those who sit in the shadow of death, is Jesus Christ, crucified and risen. No wonder, then, that we celebrate Christ's birth in the darkest time of year. But John, whose name means "the Lord is gracious," bears witness to this light, present now among us at all times, and this witness comes now to our assemblies. The Spirit of God, "the Lord and giver of life," as the Nicene Creed says, comes among us in word and sacrament and purifies our offerings to become praise of God and service to our neighbor (Heb. 13:15-16).

PETER AND PAUL, APOSTLES, JUNE 29

John 21:15-19
Acts 12:1-11
Psalm 87:1-3, 5-7 Glorious things are spoken of you, O city of our God. (Ps. 87:3)
2 Timothy 4:6-8, 17-18

Having read these readings, consider this:

The martyrdoms of Peter and Paul are not reported in the New Testament, but they are suggested. In the appendix of the Gospel according to John, the risen Jesus enables Peter to redo his threefold denial by replacing it with a threefold assertion of faithful love. Then Peter is told of his forthcoming death. In Timothy, written late in the first century, Paul is imaged as saying he has "finished the race" and he is being "poured out as a libation." These deaths reflect and point to the death of Jesus. But the accounts also bear witness in image to the resurrection of Jesus: Peter, under the threat of death, is released from prison to further feed the flock of Christ. Paul, "rescued from the lion's mouth," fully proclaims the message that all the nations might hear it. They are finally killed for being Christians, yet their joint proclamation lives on. Although the New Testament shows them as having had significant disagreements, we celebrate them here together. Around their shared witness, the city of God is built in unity. We come into that city whenever we gather in assembly under the mercy of the triune God. In baptism, we are born in that city. At eucharist, we may sing, with the psalm, "All my fresh springs are in you."

MARY, MOTHER OF OUR LORD, AUGUST 15

Luke 1:46-55
Isaiah 61:7-11
Psalm 34:1-9 Proclaim with me the greatness of the LORD. (Ps. 34:3)
Galatians 4:4-7

Having read these readings, consider this:

The mother of Jesus speaks only three times in the New Testament narratives: She says to the angel, "Let it be with me according to your word" (Luke 1:38). She prays for others, "They have no wine" (John 2:3). And she sings this robust song, a song very much like that of the restored exiles in Isaiah 61 and like the praise in today's psalm. It is no wonder that Luther considered Mary to be a type of the believer and thus a model for us. But where, in this world, are the poor lifted up and the hungry filled? Or where, to use the other readings, are the shamed clothed as for a wedding or slaves received as beloved children? We are invited to trust that in the resurrection of Jesus and in the pouring out of the Spirit—into our assemblies and into our hearts—these amazing things have begun. Let us then turn away from trying to be the proud and the powerful and, instead, join with Mary in praising the action of God, in praying for others, and in saying, "Let it be with me according to your word."

HOLY CROSS DAY, SEPTEMBER 14

John 3:13-17
Numbers 21:4b-9
Psalm 98:1-4 The LORD has done marvelous things. (Ps. 98:1)
1 Corinthians 1:18-24

Having read these readings, consider this:

We are often the ones who complain about our lot in the world. And we are bitten by many different serpents: fear, sorrow, envy, mortality. But the cross, which simply looks like more death, is actually the sign of God's love for the world, including us. The cross of Jesus, which we honor today, is wisdom for our foolishness, healing for our sorrow, forgiveness for our sin. It is God's tree of life for the healing of the nations. In the assembly, we hear the word of the cross proclaimed. We have been baptized into the death and resurrection of the Crucified One. And we eat and drink the gifts from the cross. By the inspiration of the Spirit, we look in faith and live.

MICHAEL AND ALL ANGELS, SEPTEMBER 29

Luke 10:17-20
Daniel 10:10-14; 12:1-3
Psalm 103:1-5, 20-22 Bless the LORD, you angels, all you hosts of God. (Ps. 103:20, 21)
Revelation 12:7-12

Having read these readings, consider this:

The point of this festival is not to encourage us to believe in angels and demons, but to believe in the power of *God*, a power that the Bible frequently images with the action of angelic messengers, extensions of God's mighty action in all the world. Michael's name means "Who is like God?" The implied answer to that question, a question that Israel asks us all, is "No one!" It is God who delivers the people and defeats the powers of evil. For Christians, the proclamation of the gospel causes Satan to fall. For Christians, the accuser is overcome by the blood of the Lamb. The Spirit brings us to trust that nothing is stronger than the dominion of God and the authority of the Messiah of God. Listening to the scripture, we can know that we are addressed and thus that our names are "written in the book." Then we are invited to turn to our neighbors in this troubled world with the same assurance that we have been given in Christ.

REFORMATION DAY, OCTOBER 31

John 8:31-36
Jeremiah 31:31-34
Psalm 46 The LORD of hosts is with us; the God of Jacob is our stronghold. (Ps. 46:7)
Romans 3:19-28

Having read these readings, consider this:

In what word shall we continue in order to be free? Not our own words, words we speak so often to ourselves: "I am already free; I already know the truth." No. Such assertions simply show our delusions. We need rather to continue in the word of Jesus Christ: in him we may each of us, from the least to the greatest, know God because we know God's forgiveness through Christ; he has made us a part of God's household; that house is found here in the assembly around the Crucified and Risen One and around his word; and by the power of the Spirit, we eat now the meal of the new covenant in Christ's blood. Paul—and after Paul, Luther—speaks these same matters in another way: we are justified by God's grace as a gift because of Christ, not because of our own claims and self-importance. Humility must turn us to work and pray for unity among all of God's people, not criticizing others out of our own insistence on being right, but rejoicing in the gift of the household. The danger for Lutherans of using these readings on this festival is that we may simply celebrate ourselves while dismissing other Christians and Jews. The hope of the Reformation is, rather, deep joy in the presence of the triune God in the house of which Christ has made us a member by grace.

ALL SAINTS DAY (NOVEMBER 1) OR ALL SAINTS SUNDAY

See in each year, between Lectionary 31 and Lectionary 32.